SANTA'S BOARDROOM

A Story of How a Company
Built a Beloved Brand

LISA S. LEE

LILA&COMPANY

Lila & Company
3519 NE 15th Avenue #415
Portland, OR 97212
www.lilaandcompany.com

First edition: November 2019
Print Edition ISBN: 978-1-7342030-0-4
Digital Edition ISBN: 978-1-7342030-1-1
Library of Congress Control Number: 2019918394

Illustrations by Jill Dryer
Book Design by Kate Custis

For my parents,
Won Jay Lee & Moon Jung Lee

CONTENTS

SANTA'S
BOARDROOM

A Story of How a Company
Built a Beloved Brand

AUTHOR'S NOTE

This is a marketing book. If you've picked up the book because you thought it was a children's book, you can gently set it down now. If you picked it up because you were intrigued by its title, then maybe I can offer something of value to you.

I am a brand strategist, and I've been working with brands for over twenty-five years. I've had many different jobs over my career—from an account executive at a special events marketing firm after college to running my own brand strategy firm today. I've worked on the client-side as a brand manager and on the agency-side as an account planner. Over my career, I've worked at and with some of the largest consumer brand companies—Unilever, PepsiCo, Johnson & Johnson, SC Johnson, and L'Oreal, to name a few. I conduct consumer research, write brand strategies, develop innovation concepts—all in the pursuit of developing stronger brands.

I wrote this book because I wanted to help people get better at this thing called branding. My goal is to teach you some basic marketing principles—such as the importance of target marketing, the elements of a positioning statement, and the creation of a visual identity.

I could have written a traditional "how-to" book on branding, but that didn't appeal to me. You see, I am a storyteller. I thought it would be much more interesting to explain branding concepts through a story—a story that people could relate to. That brought me to the well-known tale of Santa Claus.

Using Santa's Workshop as the backdrop for this marketing story is not meant to be a statement on religion, philosophy, or the like. I picked it because it is widely known and full of rich context and characters. Basically, it makes for a good story.

To explain the principles of branding, I changed some of the basic tenets of the story. You may not be surprised to find that the story is set in Santa's Workshop at the North Pole. But you may be surprised that this story begins in 1969, seven years after Santa's operations began. I have taken other liberties with the story, which in time you will learn.

Before you begin this story, dear reader, I have a few requests. First, please erase all of your preconceived notions about the birth of the Santa Claus legend. And second, please trust me as I take you into my version of Santa's Workshop. In time, I hope that you will discover that the creative license I took in this book was mainly to make reading the book more enjoyable, and to illustrate the merits of branding better.

I appreciate the faith you have given me in picking up this book and investing the time to read it. I sincerely hope that you learn how branding can help your business grow. And I also hope you will find it to be an entertaining read. I certainly enjoyed writing it.

So, now let's go to the North Pole and meet Santa Claus….

PROLOGUE

A lmost every child—even the littlest of children— can tell you about Santa Claus' journey every year on Christmas Eve. But while the story of Santa Claus is well known, most people are surprised to learn that several decades ago, Santa's Workshop was in jeopardy of shutting its doors. The Workshop was in danger of closing, not just for a short period, but FOREVER.

It was 1969, the same year as the moon landing—one of the most triumphant moments in human history. People from around the world watched Armstrong's moon walk on television and read about it in every newspaper the next morning. Because the press was so focused on this revolutionary event, very little was written about Santa's Workshop, so very few people knew about this dark period in the company's history.

Back then, Santa's Workshop operated very differently than it does today. In fact, Santa Claus didn't always deliver his gifts personally to children around the world, and they didn't always arrive on the same day every year. Santa Claus initially sent toys through the mail using the 'good ole reliable postal service.'

First, children asked Santa Claus for a toy either by

writing a letter or calling the North Pole. The Workshop received requests in their sophisticated consumer call center and mailroom. The staff of elves put each child's toy wish on a list and then handed out the requests to the appropriate department in the Workshop—the doll department, the wooden train group, and so on. The elves created the toys by hand, and then the gifts were packaged and shipped out to the kids. One day during the year, a child would get a toy that he himself requested in the mail.

Santa Claus started the Workshop with a vision to bring joy to children around the world. The operations of the company supported this vision for five years, and the Workshop successfully brought smiles to kids throughout these years. But after a while, things started to change. Not only did Santa want to spread joy to children, but he also wanted to spread joy to everyone—even those who did not specifically request gifts from the Workshop.

Santa began to expand his operations, and this created a lot of unforeseen challenges to his business. The Workshop developed cash flow issues from overexpansion and suffered from significant consumer perception issues. Negative public relations also threatened the Workshop's livelihood. Santa Claus' Workshop was on the brink of collapse.

At that time, Santa Claus and a courageous group of his most trusted company executives decided it was time to change the way things were done at the North Pole. Suffice it to say, the Workshop, as we know it today, may have ceased to exist if not for the brains behind the radical reinvention of Santa's Workshop. They did this by employing a disciplined branding approach to their business. It not only radically changed the way they did business, but it also revolutionized the way they looked at their products. They began viewing their business as a "brand," and it changed everything they did.

Let's go back in time to some months before Santa engaged his executives to reinvent the Workshop.

CHAPTER 1
A NEW PRODUCT IDEA

S anta arrived at the door of the workshop out of breath. Holding a drawing tightly in his fists, he headed toward the executive area on the south side of the vast building. Forgetting to brush off his black Wellies, he left a trail of snow on the workshop floor. Chief Toymaker Jacob grabbed a mop and wiped away the trail of dirty snow that Santa left in his wake.

When Santa entered the executive office, a large communal room filled with small desks, he rushed over to Georgia's desk and plopped the drawing on top of the papers she was reading.

"Hey!" she yelled as she turned around.

Santa Claus' big frame towered over her. Embarrassed, she quickly apologized, "Sorry, Santa. I thought you were someone else."

"I have the greatest idea, Georgia!" said Santa.

"Oh, really," Georgia uttered as she looked over at Simon with despair.

"A new product! I thought about this as I was watching Mrs. Claus get ready this morning. I don't know why I didn't think about this earlier. I've seen her do this every day since we've been married. That's over twenty years," he said.

Holding up the paper, Georgia examined the drawing. Sketched on a piece of white paper was an elegantly designed perfume bottle with the words "Santa's Scent" written in cursive on the label.

"What do you think?" asked Santa as Simon walked over to Georgia and looked at the drawing over her shoulder. Georgia turned the paper sideways, upside down, and then held it up close to her face to examine the details. Santa waited eagerly for an answer.

"It's nice," she said, handing it back to him. "But we can't produce it here at the Workshop."

"What do you mean? It's simple to make. It's just a bottle. We have the best craftsmen in the world at the North Pole. Right, Simon?"

"To tell you the truth, Santa," Simon said as he crossed his arms, "Georgia's right. We mainly use wood and plastic in the workshop. Glass production requires expensive kilns and raw materials that we don't have. I don't think our craftsmen know anything about blowing intricate glass like this. We'd have to bring in a glassblower who knows how to do this."

"As I said, we can't do this," Georgia said as she turned back to her work. She had a line of new dolls that she needed to put into production that week.

But Santa was not ready to give up on his idea. "But you are one of the smartest product developers I know. I know you can figure out a way to do this—even if it takes some investment. I think we can find some money in our budget to do this efficiently. Right, Simon?"

"Don't take this the wrong way," Simon replied, "but

expanding into underwear and socks last year really killed our profit margin. We don't have the capital to make the kind of investment needed for this type of product."

"You make it sound like it was a mistake to expand," Santa said. "These weren't any 'ole underwear and socks. They're super durable and they're the longest lasting ones available. They beat the socks off of everything on the market today!"

Georgia said, treading lightly, "Santa, when you recruited us to help you create Santa's Workshop, you told us that you wanted to bring joy to children around the world."

"Yes, that's right," said Santa. "At least you're listening to me."

"Well, I'm just wondering how underwear and socks help bring joy."

"People need underwear and socks. Can you imagine? You just got a hole in your socks. And then in the mail, you get a brand new, beautiful pair of long-lasting wool socks. That would delight so many people." Santa was tickled with happiness.

"But do children really need socks to last ten years? Aren't their feet constantly growing?" asked Simon.

"That's not the point," said Santa dismissively.

"And last year, you asked us to expand to adult underwear and socks, and then we added women's handbags and men's ties," Georgia reminded Santa.

"And don't forget women's accessories," added Simon.

"I thought we were going to focus on kids, and now we're making all these products for adults," said Georgia. "What are your corporate sponsors going to say if we keep moving away from our core market of children?" Since the toys were financed by the companies that licensed Santa's image for children's products, they had to consider whether these companies would favorably view this new line.

"Everyone needs a little joy, don't you think?" Santa sang sweetly. "In fact, Georgia, I think you need a little joy. How about a sleigh ride with me? Won't that make you feel better?"

Feeling exasperated, Georgia shook her head. "I don't need a sleigh ride. I need you to understand the potential issues this will bring. The capital investment will be high. Inventory and material costs will be high. And we'd have to implement new job training."

"What if we bought the glass in bulk and had it labeled here?" asked Simon.

"But everything here is handmade," said Santa.

Simon gave Georgia a look of defeat. Simon didn't want to disappoint Santa. But he was a pragmatist, and he knew this idea was not a good one for the company.

"Georgia, you are a great developer, and Simon, you are the best financial expert I know. The two of you can definitely figure out a way to make these beautiful perfume bottles."

Santa often sang praises to his executives, which made it hard for them to say no to him. Georgia wore a gloomy, hopeless look in her eyes. In her head, Georgia knew she could find a way to make Santa's perfume bottles, but in her heart, she also knew it wasn't the best thing for the Workshop.

Georgia gave Santa a weak smile and then asked, "How much perfume do you want in each bottle?"

"Whatever you recommend!" Santa bellowed. He handed

the sketch back to Georgia. As he walked away, he began to laugh with joy. Santa's "ho, ho, ho" could be heard across the workshop floor until the door slammed shut behind him.

CHAPTER 2
THE MAKING OF
A PERFUME

Georgia picked up the sketch again and studied it carefully. The bottle design was intricate and delicate, like Venetian glass. A bottle like this would need to be developed by a very experienced glassblower.

"Georgia, I don't like it either…but we'll figure out a way to make this work." Simon took the drawing from Georgia and studied it.

"I know we can figure it out," said Georgia. "I just feel like we're expanding too quickly, and we have no direction. I loved the idea of bringing joy to children around the world. That's why I decided to take this job. But now, he wants to bring joy to everyone. We can't possibly do that."

"You know Santa. He thinks big. He always has. Bringing joy to everyone is his new vision," said Simon, torn about his concern for the financial stability of the company and his loyalty to Santa. Trying to be optimistic, he said, "Look, we can get Melinda to help put the feelers out in New York for someone who can help us set up this perfume line."

"And where are we going to find a Nose?" she asked.

"A Nose?"

"You know…a person who can put together scents for a perfume—a perfumer," she answered. "That's a very specialized skill. And how do we find an elf to do that work? If we hire a human, we'll have to retool all the workspaces to be human-sized. And then we'll have to figure out..."

"Okay, okay. We'll cross that bridge when we get there," Simon assured her. "Right now, we need to find the right person. I'll call Melinda, and then I'll get on the phone with some people I know in Paris...we'll start from there."

They got back to their desks and began making calls. The wheels were in motion to develop Santa's Scent, a new line of perfume for women.

There was so much to think about in launching this new item. Not only did the team have design issues to contend with, like how to create the delicate glass bottle and develop a unique scent, but they also had to figure out how to fit it within their production schedule. Due to the complexity of the product, these items would take four times the amount of time it would take to make their most intricate toy. And this was contingent on finding a highly skilled glassblower and perfumer. Then there was the cost of purchasing and maintaining a large kiln that the glassblower would use to create the bottles. The Workshop would also need to carry a large inventory of glass rods for the glass production and new ingredients for the creation of the scent. Also, they had to create original packaging for the fragile item, one that safeguarded the product during shipping.

They took all of these challenges to heart and tackled them one by one. And after many production meetings and phone calls with suppliers and machine makers, the line was ready to run in a record three months. The elves' workspaces were rearranged to make way for the shiny, new equipment they had purchased from a French manufacturer.

Georgia and Ethan, the head of Human Resources, spent hours interviewing the right candidates for the two positions. They spoke with humans and elves alike. The human candidates were real glassblowers and perfumers, and Ethan and Georgia were thrilled to find such high caliber candidates. The candidates, on the other hand, were less than pleased when they arrived at the North Pole on an exceedingly cold winter day surrounded by elves half their size and a village made in elf proportions. When the human candidates returned home to the comfort of their own human-sized homes, all of them respectfully withdrew their candidacy for the two available jobs.

That left the elf candidates, who, for the most part, were not as experienced as the human candidates. The most experienced elf they found for the glassblower job was a craftsman by the name of Oona. Though her specialty was not glassblowing, she was an expert potter who made an impressive array of beautiful pots. Oona convinced Ethan and Georgia that she could do glassblowing equally as well.

They were unable to find an elf who specialized in perfumes because elves did not wear perfume, but they did find a chef who had a wonderful sense of smell and a flare for inventiveness when it came to his food. Chef Milo even came personally recommended by their own Chef Aaron, the chef of their dining hall. He was the near-perfect candidate for the job.

When the new hires arrived and settled into the North Pole, Santa hosted a ceremony to welcome them to the company. Then he presided over the ribbon-cutting ceremony for the new glassblowing space on the workshop floor. Santa beamed with joy as he slashed the red ribbon and welcomed in a new era to Santa's Workshop. As he looked around the workshop at the elves, he wished that they too could feel his delight.

CHAPTER 3
IN PRODUCTION

Just one month into their new production schedule, problems were already arising. When they were producing only toys, production was steady. But when they added the garment manufacturing line, it slowed down the Workshop's overall throughput. The socks, underwear, and ties were handmade, and therefore, required elves to spin cotton, make fabric, and then sew the material into the appropriate garment. The addition of the perfume operations added a whole level of complexity that slowed down production even more.

Chef Milo, while possessing complementary job skills, was far from a perfumer. Mixing essences to create a scent was vastly different from cooking food and developing diverse flavor profiles. It took him a long time to learn how to formulate interesting scents. He went through fifty liters of essences before he could find a formula he was happy with, and even then, it required ten different ingredients that they needed to have on hand at all times. Simon tried to convince Chef Milo to change the formulation since the essences he had chosen for the perfume were extremely expensive, but Chef Milo could not. He would not compromise, because any change to his formula would be an insult to his artistry.

Likewise, Oona was not a professional glassblower. She went through 851 rods before she was able to replicate Santa's design, and even then, it wasn't exact. It took the two new hires four months to produce the very first bottle of perfume from Santa's Workshop, even after the line was ready to run.

Over the four months, resentment over the perfume line grew and grew. Because it took up a lot of space, the elves had to make their toys and garments in a smaller area on the factory floor. The heat from the kiln was unbearable at times, particularly by the afternoon when the oven had been running for several hours. The elves also complained about the sticky-sweet scents from the perfume-making station. Ethan and Georgia tried to improve the situation by bringing in fans to get rid of the smell and the heat, but the noise from the fans bothered the elves even more.

The overcrowding, the heat, and the noise began to affect the elves' productivity. The executive team had to increase everyone's hours to make their production goals for the month. They had already missed their production numbers for the last four months, and if they didn't meet their monthly production goals, they would be severely behind in fulfilling kids' wishes. The list was getting longer and longer each month. Extending everyone's hours was the only option.

Chief Toymaker Jacob came into the executive office and found Simon and Georgia at their desks. "If we continue at this pace, the elves are going to get burnt out," he said. "These conditions are deplorable, and now you are requiring them to work ten-hour shifts. This is un-elf-like!"

"Jacob," Simon said, "I know this is hard. But the hours will decrease once we become more efficient. We all have to work harder right now. Even the executives are putting in twelve-hour days to manage the complexity of the new operations."

Jacob didn't look reassured. After he left, Georgia turned to Simon and said, "Well, one thing that would help is to get Santa off these ridiculous new products. If we weren't so diversified, we could handle the workload. I told you making perfume was a bad idea!"

"Okay, I see your point. There's no use complaining to each other. Let's set up a meeting with Santa and tell him what's going on. He'll listen," said Simon.

CHAPTER 4
AN INTERVENTION

The next day, Georgia, Simon, and Ethan set up a meeting, or rather an intervention, with Santa. At Santa's house, which contained his living quarters as well as his office, the executives summoned Santa into the boardroom adjacent to his office, where they met regularly for weekly production and status meetings. As usual, Santa sat at the head of the old oak table, and the executives each took their regular seats—Georgia to his right, Simon to his left, and Ethan next to Simon.

"Why so formal everyone?" asked Santa.

"This is an official business meeting…an important one," Simon said. The executives had stayed up most of the night, pulling together a presentation on the current state of the Workshop. Simon opened the presentation with an overview of the financial state of the Workshop. He led Santa through the revenue figures of current licensees and the expense numbers—material and labor costs, delivery charges, and marketing-related expenses. "We are barely breaking even, Santa. But that's not the scariest thing. One change in any of these numbers and the Workshop is in serious trouble. If we lose one of our licensees, we won't survive another month. Our material costs are the highest they've been in years. If it continues to increase, we will be in a very precarious situation."

"That's not the only thing," said Georgia. "We are not yet fully operational with the perfume line, and it's already slowing the overall throughput of the factory. When it does become fully operational, according to Simon's scenario, we could experience a major financial meltdown."

Santa stared at Simon's bar charts and pie charts in the report in front of him. "Well, we'll have to make sure that none of that happens."

"We need to have a contingency plan, just in case any of those scenarios happen," said Simon.

"You worry too much, Simon. The Workshop will be fine!" said Santa, adding a big belly laugh.

"Santa," Ethan chimed in. "The numbers are not the only thing. We are wearing out our employees. They have been putting in ten-hour days just to keep up with production, and even then, we are falling short. The elves are complaining about their workload. I've been overhearing conversations in the lunchroom, and they're not happy."

"Don't they know that we're trying to spread joy? Isn't that enough to motivate them to work hard?" Santa asked.

"The elves are questioning our strategy. They think we've lost sight of what we're doing. They're wondering why we're making all these things," Georgia explained.

"Because we want to spread joy!" Santa exclaimed. "I want to bring smiles to people all over the world."

"We started by making presents for children, but now we are giving gifts to everyone. Why everyone?" Georgia said, treading lightly.

"Look how much despair there is in the world! There is a cold war going on. Countries are fighting. People are scared that a nuclear war will end the world. That's why we need to spread joy. We have to bring happiness back to this world!" Santa took a deep breath. "I know you're all concerned, but I think we're doing great. I would hate to cut back on anything right now because, while it's a little uncomfortable at the moment, we are still spreading joy."

The three elves looked at each other from across the boardroom table, unsure of what to do. Georgia began to say, "But Santa..."

"Enough," he interrupted. "I don't want to hear it. We are Santa's Workshop, and we have an important mission to fulfill in this world." The conversation ended when Santa got up from the table and returned to his office.

"That went well," Ethan said sarcastically.

"This could be bad. We'll have to hope we don't have any mishaps. We can't afford even a small margin of error," said Simon.

Santa's top three executives gathered their papers from the table and then walked slowly back to their offices with their heads held low.

CHAPTER 5
THE PHONE CALL

A few weeks later, Georgia received an urgent call from Melinda, the company's head public relations representative in New York.

"Georgia. Bad news. I've received some intelligence from my guys on the street. They say that people are donating their gifts from Santa to charities. The Salvation Army and Goodwill both reported receiving Santa's Workshop ties, purses, and perfumes in large numbers across the country. I called our offices in Amsterdam, Beijing, São Paolo, and Nairobi, and they say the same thing is happening in their markets."

"Are you sure, Melinda? Are you sure they're Santa's gifts?"

"I'm positive. The products have Santa's Workshop labels on them," she said firmly. "That's not the only thing. My contacts in the press have heard rumors that Santa is running a sweatshop in the North Pole. They say that the elves are working ridiculous hours. Two of our major licensees are talking about pulling out of their agreements due to these rumors. If any of these newspapers or magazines run a bad story about the Workshop, we'll be in serious trouble. The rumors aren't true, are they?"

Georgia fumbled with her words, "Melinda, we're having some issues with production. But we're trying to sort things out. Give me a few days, and I'll get back to you with our plan."

"Listen, Georgia, maybe you should bring someone in to help you think through the Workshop's strategy? I know someone here in New York, a brand strategist. She could work with Santa and the team to turn this around," Melinda offered.

"What's a brand strategist?"

"A brand strategist is someone who can help us think about how to improve the health of our brand. She can help us position our brand for growth," she explained.

Georgia was too busy thinking about the repercussions of Melinda's news to ask more questions. She scribbled the name and number of the brand strategist on a piece of paper and then tacked it onto her corkboard.

"Thanks, Melinda. I'll call you in two days," she said and then hung up the phone.

CHAPTER 6
EMERGENCY MEETING

Having overheard the call, Simon said, "I think it's time for an emergency meeting."

"I'll meet you in ten minutes in Santa's office," Georgia said as she grabbed her coat and went searching for Ethan.

After searching North Pole Village, Georgia finally located Ethan in the reindeer barn. Ethan was talking to Reindeer Master Aidan about making room for a new reindeer. A reindeer baby would be born in three months. They were excited about the new addition and tried to engage Georgia in their enthusiasm, but Georgia was too concerned with the news to make idle chit chat. Instead, Georgia rushed Ethan to Santa's office, where Simon was already waiting outside the door.

"Okay. Let's make sure we don't sound too alarmist," Simon said to his two colleagues.

"But this is dire, Simon. We could be closed in a few months!"

"Don't say that, Georgia," Ethan said. "What would all the elves do? What would we do? And what would happen to all those people? They won't be able to experience that joyful feeling of getting a gift from Santa's Workshop."

"Don't worry," Simon assured them. "We just need to put on our thinking caps, and we'll figure this out. Let's just tell Santa the situation. Our goal is to get him to commit to solving this as a team. Okay?"

Georgia and Ethan nodded their heads. The three executives entered Santa's home, where Mrs. Claus was baking cookies in the kitchen.

"Oh, good!" Mrs. Claus exclaimed. "You can taste my new recipe for snowflake cookies. I even made a version for the reindeer. Don't they look cute?"

They nodded in agreement as Mrs. Claus showed them the snowflake-shaped cookies covered with white frosting and shimmery silver sprinkles. "Oh, yes, very cute," "Good enough to eat," "Looks delicious," sang the executives.

"We have important business with Santa," Simon said diplomatically to excuse themselves.

"He's in his office." Mrs. Claus pointed to the door. "Oh, bring a plate of these in with you, please," she said as she gave Ethan a plate of snowflake cookies. Ethan surreptitiously slid a cookie off of the plate and into his mouth.

Simon knocked on the door and led the three executives into Santa's office. Ethan placed the cookies on the edge of Santa's desk and then resumed his place in line with his colleagues in front of the desk.

"What a pleasure! And you brought cookies. Mrs. Claus is trying to spoil me!" Santa said, reaching out for a cookie.

Simon spoke first. "Santa, we have some bad news."

"Bad news. There is no bad news in Santa's Village. Everything here is perfect, just like I imagined it." Santa sat back in his chair and gave out a belly laugh. He looked at the photo hanging on the wall. It was taken on the day that he, Simon, and Georgia had arrived by reindeer carriage at the North Pole seven years ago. It was the day he purchased over a thousand acres of land at the northernmost tip of the world. "Remember that photo? The Workshop was just a dream back then, and now look at this place," he said as he waved his arms around the room.

"It could be gone tomorrow," said Simon.

Georgia nudged Simon with her elbow. "I thought you said we weren't going to alarm him."

"I lied," he said to Georgia under his breath. "Santa," he said matter-of-factly, "If we don't change things around here, we're in jeopardy of closing."

"Closing?" said Santa. "That's ridiculous. Why would we close?"

Georgia stepped in, "I got a call from Melinda in New York. People are donating our gifts to charity."

"And they're re-gifting them too," said Ethan, his mouth still full of cookies.

"That's not all. There are rumors that you're running a sweatshop and the elves are not happy," Georgia added.

"Our sponsors may pull out because of these rumors," Simon said. "Remember what I told you, Santa? If any of our licensees pull out, we are done."

"Si-ya-nara," said Ethan.

"Adios," said Georgia.

"Caput," added Simon.

Santa sat back in his large black office chair. "Finished? We just started. Why would people be sending back our presents? They are finely crafted items."

"Clearly, Santa, these gifts are not what they want," Georgia answered, holding back the "I told you so" commentary.

"Why would they think we're running a sweatshop? Our elves are happy, aren't they?"

"Well, I tried to tell you before," Ethan said carefully. "The elves think they're being overworked."

"They are miserable," Simon said. "They're working like dogs. They don't know why we're making so many different products. They don't understand our strategy. They think we've lost our way. There is no joy at Santa's Workshop."

"No joy?" Santa said, bewildered. The words felt like icicle daggers in his heart. "How could that be? I've worked so hard to make everyone happy." He sat in his chair, silent for quite some time. The three executives stood in front of Santa quietly as he pondered the situation.

Simon finally broke the silence. "I suggest, Santa, that we meet tomorrow morning to strategize on what to do to turn the Workshop around."

"We are all here—a hundred percent, Santa," said Georgia.

"You can count on us," Ethan said. "Santa's Workshop will bring joy to everyone once again."

Santa was touched by the elves' enthusiasm, but he was still shocked by the news. It was difficult for him to feel equally hopeful. He was both saddened and panicked by the news that Santa's Workshop was no longer filled with joy. It was bad enough that people around the world were rejecting his gifts, but the hardest truth to digest was the fact that his employees were not happy.

"Okay. Let's start tomorrow at nine a.m." Santa could barely look at the executives when he spoke. "We'll meet in the boardroom."

The three elves filed out of Santa's office one by one. As they left, Santa said under his breath, "Have a joyful evening."

CHAPTER 7
THE FIRST BOARD MEETING

At nine a.m. the next morning, the executives arrived at Santa's boardroom for the start of what was to become known as the reinvention of Santa's Workshop. Mrs. Claus had made homemade blueberry muffins and chocolate chip scones, as well as a large pot of coffee, and left them in the center of the large oak table. The table, Santa's pride and joy, was handcrafted from a two-hundred-year-old oak that had been logged in Canada. The elves and Santa took their usual seats around the old oak table, with Santa at the head.

"I asked Melinda to join us by conference call," announced Georgia.

"That's great. I haven't talked to Melinda since our last executive meeting," Santa said.

Georgia dialed Melinda's phone number on the conference phone while Ethan helped himself to two scones and a muffin. There was a click on the other end of the phone and the sound of a familiar voice, "Santa's Workshop. This is Melinda."

"Melinda!" bellowed Santa. "How are you? We miss you here in the North Pole. When are you going to come and visit?"

"Well, soon enough, I hope. We are having a bit of a crisis down here. When things quiet down, I'm hoping to make it up for a visit."

"Yes. The team tells me that people are re-gifting and donating our gifts. Why is that? We think so carefully about what we produce. Why don't they like our products?"

"Well, Santa, we've been talking to the donation centers, and they say people don't see any use for these gifts," she answered.

"No use?" Santa said.

"Well, for example, a lot of men's ties are being donated. The volunteers who run the donation centers tell me that ties reflect a man's personality. Some guys like to wear bright pink ties with their suits, and others like to wear pinstripes. So, the ties that are being donated don't fit the man and his style. Does that make sense?"

"I'm a red suit kind of guy," Santa said, giving out a chuckle. The others around the table laughed with him.

Melinda continued, "And with perfume...that's a special kind of gift. A woman spends years finding her perfect scent. It's not something she likes to get as a gift unless it's something that she buys all the time. It's very...you know... personal."

"Santa, I hate to say this...but I told you expanding wasn't a good idea," Georgia said, ignoring Simon's disapproving look.

"And they think we're running a sweatshop." Melinda's last word rang through the conference room as the group fell quiet.

"A sweatshop," Santa said somberly.

"Whatever you call it, Santa, the elves are disgruntled," Ethan said. He quickly shuffled through the disorganized stack of papers in front of him and pulled out a piece of paper. "Last night, I polled the elves to try and understand what was driving the low employee morale. I prepared a synopsis of the research. Sorry, Melinda, we'll fax you a copy. I didn't know you'd be joining us. Just listen along." Ethan passed out the one-page report to everyone at the table. "According to the poll, on a scale of one to ten—where one is miserable, and ten is extreme joy—they rated working at the Workshop a three."

"A three?" Santa said in disbelief.

"A three," he repeated.

Santa looked out the window that overlooked the village square. Santa's silence seemed as long as an eternal summer day at the North Pole. The executives looked at each other, afraid to speak.

Finally, Georgia spoke, attempting to reassure Santa. "We'll get that back to a ten, Santa."

"At least we now know where we're starting and where we need to go," said Simon.

"Is there anything else?" asked Santa.

"Well, we asked them the reasons they were not feeling joy," Ethan continued, referring to the summary report he held in his hand. "The top reasons are that they feel overworked, and they don't have a purpose, or in other words, they don't know why they're making the gifts."

"What do you mean they don't know why they are making the gifts? To spread joy! We've always been about spreading joy!" said Santa.

"I'm just reporting the results," Ethan said in a hushed voice.

"Ethan, it's okay. Just continue," said Simon.

"And, finally, another reason is they don't know what the vision of the Workshop is."

"Vision...We are supposed to spread joy to everyone!" Santa banged his fist onto the old oak table. His hard work over the last seven years was being questioned, and his heart was beginning to ache.

"Perhaps," said Melinda cautiously. "Perhaps that's too lofty of a vision for the elves. Maybe they need to see that their work is really having an impact on the people they're making these products for."

"What do you mean? We've been making people happy for years now," Santa said defensively.

"I think what Melinda is saying is that the elves don't feel connected to the people who use our products," explained Georgia. "They feel like they are just making products...not spreading joy."

CHAPTER 8
CONSUMERS MATTER

"**C**an I be provocative?" asked Melinda. When nobody answered immediately, she continued. "I'd argue that we actually don't know our consumers, especially if they are returning our gifts."

Melinda's voice rang through the chilly boardroom.

"Don't know our consumers! Of course, we know them," Santa uttered with great agitation. "Mrs. Claus says that she loves our signature perfume."

"Family and friends are not consumers," said Georgia tentatively. "Melinda is right…we don't know what people south of the North Pole want. We only know what we want them to want."

"But everyone needs underwear and socks!"

"People need them, but do we really think that they're gifts that bring them joy?" asked Georgia.

Ethan thought about this for a moment. "Chocolate pudding made by Mrs. Claus, these scones, and my teddy bear… that brings me joy. Underwear brings me…I don't know… utility?"

"Utility?" Santa Claus sat back in his seat, reflecting on what his executives were saying. He couldn't help but feel attacked. After all, these innovations were *his* ideas. "Well, it certainly brings me joy to know that people have a clean pair of underwear and socks. That's what my grandma used to say to me all the time, 'Always have clean underwear and socks on!'"

"But with all due respect, sir, what you think doesn't really matter. It's what our consumers think that matters," Melinda's voice rang over the phone. She was glad that she couldn't see the faces on the other side of the phone. She knew she had to be bold to get her point across. The corporate sponsors were her responsibility; her job was on the line if any of them decided to pull out of their sponsorship agreements.

The room went silent.

Santa looked out at Simon, Georgia, and Ethan. Ethan concentrated on the scone on his plate and ate with intensity. Trying to avoid Santa's disappointing gaze, Georgia began doodling in her notebook. Simon's pen started to tap nervously on his notepad over the silence.

"I'm sorry...Did I say something to offend anyone?" Melinda's voice rang through the cold room.

CHAPTER 9
THE STRATEGIST

"**S**imon, you are quiet. What do you think of all this?" asked Santa.

"I think we have some major issues to work out, and we're not going to solve this right here, right now," Simon said.

"If I may," Georgia began, "Santa, perhaps we are too close to this. Melinda knows of a brand strategist who can help us think about how to strengthen our brand."

"A brand strategist? What's that?"

Melinda explained, "A brand strategist is a branding expert. My friend Suzie here works for one of the largest consumer food companies in the United States, and she highly recommends her. Suzie hired her to rebrand one of the oldest food brands in America. Her name is Amanda. She would help us get aligned around what Santa and the Workshop means. I think it will really help us think about who we should be targeting and what businesses we should be in."

"A brand strategist? We're not a brand...we're Santa's Workshop," said Santa.

"People don't technically 'buy' our products. But we are a brand that relies on our consumers being happy," Melinda explained.

"Yes, and I spoke with her yesterday," Georgia added. "And she explained to me that most companies, even non-profit organizations, make the mistake of thinking they're not a brand. But if we want to really impact consumers' lives and have them love us…we need to start thinking of ourselves as a brand."

"I disagree, Georgia. I think we need to look at the numbers," said Simon. "They will tell us everything. I didn't want to say this before, but maybe we should cut our perfume line now and cut our losses."

"No…no…we are not cutting production. Not yet." said Santa. "And we don't need to have someone else telling us what to do!" Santa crossed his arms and sat back in his seat.

"That's not what she's going to do," explained Melinda. "She's going to have us do the work. We'll be making all the decisions. She insists that we do the work because she knows that's the only way it will be implemented."

"We need to do something…We can't just continue to do things the way we've been doing them," said Georgia.

"I'm game if everyone else is game," said Ethan as he eyed the plate of scones in the middle of the table.

"I don't think branding is going to help us," said Simon.

Everyone looked at Santa.

"We built this place together…without an outsider's help, might I add," Santa said passionately. "We can do this on our own."

CHAPTER 10
THE INCIDENT

T he large wooden door to the workshop flung open and made a loud thump against the outside of the building. Two elves stomped out with their fists held high and their voices full of fury. Elves poured out of the workshop behind them and assembled around the dueling elves in the far corner of the village square.

Having taken notice of the yelling, the executives gathered around the boardroom window to watch the commotion. Only Santa remained seated, absorbed in thought. The list of problems at the company ran through his head like a broken record. He didn't know how he was going to lead the elves out of this business calamity. Outside, the shouting intensified.

"You took the material I was going to use for my doll," yelled Doll Maker Elijah to Ana.

"Well, you weren't using it," said Ana. "Plus, your doll is hideous."

Then a snowball came out of the crowd and hit Ana right in the face. Enraged, she picked up a snowball and threw it at Elijah. The elves watching from the sidelines took sides, hurling snowballs at each other. The snowball fight quickly escalated into an all-out war.

Just then, the door of the boardroom swung open, and Chief Toymaker Jacob burst into the room.

"Come quick. There was a fight in the workshop, and everyone is in an uproar," Jacob said out of breath.

"What happened?" asked Santa pushing himself out of his seat.

"What's going on over there?" said Melinda over the phone.

"A fight…" Jacob said. Catching his breath, he began babbling. "First, Christine accused Caleb of not pulling his weight. Then Owen accused Sally of being too slow…and then Elijah got mad at Ana for taking his materials. Oh my! What are we going to do?"

All the executives looked at Santa for the answer. "What are we going to do?" rang in Santa's ear loud and clear.

Santa put on his red coat lined with white fur and headed for the door while buckling the belt to his jacket.

Jacob ran out the door past him and yelled back, "Hurry, Santa!"

"Hello…can someone tell me what's going on?" Melinda's voice boomed over the phone speaker.

Santa stopped in the doorway and turned to Georgia. "Call this brand strategist, and let's start right away." He turned to the phone on the old oak table and raised his voice, "Melinda, you need to come up and help us turn this place around."

Then Santa left the room in a hurry, followed by Ethan. From the window of the boardroom, Georgia and Simon watched as Santa walked from the office across the path leading to the village square. When the elves finally took notice of Santa's presence, the fighting came to a halt. Santa gathered everyone around him to give a few words of encouragement.

Georgia and Simon looked at each other, knowing what the other was thinking. They didn't want to miss Santa's speech, and most of all, they wanted to make sure Santa didn't make any promises that he couldn't keep. Grabbing their coats along the way, they ran out into the village square.

"Uh, hello…What's going on?" Melinda's voice echoed through the empty boardroom. "Is anyone there?"

CHAPTER 11
SANTA'S ASSURANCE

Santa stood in front of the old North Pole sign and spoke earnestly to the belligerent elves. "Ethan has filled me in on the state of the Workshop. I have heard your concerns about the direction of the company. I want you to know that I am going to do everything I can to fix this. I'll be working with the management team to develop a new vision for the company."

As quickly as the snowballs had been thrown, questions and comments began to volley toward Santa.

"What's going to happen? Are we going to lose our jobs?"

"Why have our hours increased so much!"

"It's hot in the workshop, and that perfume smell is killing me."

"When is this going to happen?"

"Fast, I hope!"

Santa listened patiently to the questions and complaints of the elves and addressed them as diplomatically as he could. He assured them that no one was going to lose their job and that the hours would soon go back to normal once they solved the issues with the perfume production. They would address the perfume smell with a new ventilation system. Everything, he said, would take place as quickly as possible.

When it appeared that the elves were satisfied with his answers, Santa asked them to put their trust in his executive team and go back to work. Paying heed to Santa's request, the elves filed back into the workshop, returning quietly to their workbenches. The last elf to return to work closed the large wooden doors to the building.

Santa turned to Ethan and held his head low. "I had no idea things had gotten so bad."

"I guess it takes a good snowball fight to get the message across loud and clear."

"Well, I'm sorry, Ethan. I'll try to be a better listener," Santa said. "Sometimes, I just get so enthusiastic about our mission that I can't think of much else."

Ethan bid farewell to Santa and watched him walk away, the usual spring in Santa's step all but gone. Then he returned to the workshop to see what the elves thought of Santa's talk. With his clipboard in hand, Ethan walked the workshop floor and watched as the elves worked diligently at their stations. He stopped to chat with the elves and was pleased to learn that they had faith that things would get better. They loved Santa and were devoted to him—that was supremely clear. But while things appeared to be calm, Ethan knew that it was just a matter of time before another outburst occurred. He knew that the executives could really make a difference and turn things around, but he wondered if they'd be able to save the Workshop in time.

CHAPTER 12
THE CHOCOLATE HOTEL

Just one week after that defining board meeting, Melinda and Amanda arrived at the North Pole. The exact date was May 2, 1969, a seasonably cold spring day. Having taken a long chartered flight from a small Canadian town in Nunavut, the two women arrived exhausted. But because they had a few hours of light left in the day, Melinda insisted on introducing Amanda to the peculiarities of the North Pole.

First, they checked into the Chocolate Hotel, the only hotel for out-of-town guests in the North Pole. It was designed and developed by leading architect Jack Silvers and was intended for guests on official state visits. Because the village measured a mere two-mile footprint, they were not able to accommodate a large number of tourists. Permission to visit the North Pole was only granted to journalists, foreign dignitaries, and special guests, such as Amanda. Santa was always being asked to expand the hotel and open the North Pole to visitors, particularly to kids who wanted to meet the famous man. But Santa didn't like the fanfare. He also wanted the Workshop to remain in children's imagination, so any suggestions to expand the village and improve its amenities were always turned down.

In the lobby of the Chocolate Hotel, the smell of Mrs. Claus' famous warm chocolate chip cookies filled the air. Mrs. Claus' chocolate chip cookie recipe was top secret. Over the years, many guests and famous chefs have tried to replicate it, without success. The hotel served the famous cookies, a treat reserved only for hotel guests, with milk every afternoon.

When Melinda and Amanda checked into the hotel, they received their room keys. On each of their key rings was a different chocolate proverb. Amanda's read: "He who loves chocolate, loves life." She couldn't agree more with the statement because, by definition, Amanda was a chocoholic. Melinda's quote said, "Chocolate is to the soul as the sun is to the earth." They took their keys and bags with them to the elevator.

When Amanda opened her door, she was happy to discover that the room was built for humans. She sunk into the bed, wishing she could take a nap, but she had promised Melinda that they would meet in the lobby shortly. She freshened up, put on a down jacket, and then took the elevator back to the first floor.

CHAPTER 13
A TOUR OF THE NORTH POLE

"**I**'m so glad you're here!" Georgia exclaimed when Melinda and Amanda walked into her office. Georgia and Melinda shared a big hug.

Melinda had worked for Georgia for four years before she moved to New York, so they knew each other very well. Everything Melinda knew about product development, she learned from Georgia, and she owed much of her professional success to Georgia's mentorship. When the Workshop became more visible in the press, and they began expanding their operations, Santa promoted Melinda to the role of PR director. He sent her to New York City to build a worldwide network of public relations experts and to oversee their corporate sponsorships.

When Melinda introduced the women, Amanda leaned over to shake Georgia's hand. "Oh, I've heard so much about you!" exclaimed Georgia. "I hope you can help us save the Workshop."

Amanda looked around the small office and thought of how dainty and small everything was. She couldn't help but notice the wall next to Georgia's desk. Pinned to the wall hung hand-drawn pieces of paper—from large artists sheets to small napkins. "Oh, those are all of Santa's inventions,"

Georgia explained as Amanda perused the drawings of electrical miniature airplanes, fancy women's digital watches, and solar-powered bicycles. "Not all of them were made, but they are quite imaginative, wouldn't you say?"

"He's got a very creative mind," said Amanda as she studied the drawings.

"A little too creative if you ask me," said Georgia. She grabbed her wool jacket from the hook behind the door. "We better get going if we are going to take advantage of the last hour of sunshine."

Georgia began their tour of the North Pole right outside her door. She started on the workshop floor, where the toys, underwear, socks, handbags, ties, and perfume were made. The workstations were organized into rows, and each row represented a different production line. As they passed each work area, Amanda and Melinda watched the master craftsmen work quickly by hand.

On the train-making line, one elf cut wooden pieces from a slab of lumber on a jigsaw and handed off the cut pieces to another elf to sand them down. The wood pieces went to an elf who painted them and to another elf who drilled holes into each piece. The final elf attached the wheels and the sliding doors to the locomotive cab and then placed the completed toy train into a bin.

When the women reached the end of the train-making line, Georgia offered to take the bin of finished trains to the mailroom. Georgia pushed the cart through the workshop floor as Amanda and Melinda tried to keep up with the fast-moving cart. When they arrived in the mailroom, the bin was left in a holding station where it entered the mailing process.

At the first station, an elf took a train out of the cart and wrapped it in tissue. At the second station, the train was placed into a box. At the third station, it was covered with brown paper, and at the fourth station, the box was addressed to the recipient. Finally, the package went into a holding area to wait for the mail truck that arrived every other morning at 10 a.m.

"You have really amazing operations," marveled Amanda, as they left the workshop. "I've been to many factories. I thought the breakfast cereal plant was fun…but this is by far the best."

The women walked through the village square, which was modeled after a ski village in Switzerland. Shops lined the square where the elves could spend their hard-earned money on anything from candy to electronics. The newsstand sold items like stationery, film, and newspapers. A small market carried fresh vegetables, meat, and canned goods, and some special elf delicacies like chocolate-covered wild raspberries and lembas, thin bread-like cakes wrapped in leaves. The most impressive store was the Mega Store, a department store stocked with all sorts of goods, from blankets to music records.

Right in the main square was a doorway that led to a large dining hall where the elves ate three meals a day. The famous Chef Aaron was in charge of the dining hall, which everyone referred to as 'the cantina.' He took great pride in serving the most delicious meals north of the equator. Mealtime was undoubtedly the highlight of the elves' day.

After their tour of the dining hall, Georgia brought them

to see the reindeer barn. She had arranged for Aidan, the reindeer's caretaker, to take the women on an evening sleigh ride so that they could experience the magic of these beautiful creatures.

"How delightful!" exclaimed Amanda as the carriage pulled by four flying reindeer lifted off the ground. Skillfully guiding the sleigh through the air, Aidan gave the women an aerial tour of North Pole Village and the surrounding area.

First, Aidan flew the carriage toward the Castle, the large dormitory modeled after a French castle that housed the living quarters for all the elves. As Aidan led the reindeer back south toward the Village, the carriage floated through the air as if riding on smooth, soft waves in the ocean.

"Oh, wow…there's the workshop! And there's the reindeer barn," Amanda pointed out. As she looked into the horizon, a vast white blanket of snow stretched for miles beyond Santa's Village. The very beginning of the Canadian Rocky Mountains could be seen in the distance.

That day, the sky was crystal clear, and the sun was just beginning to set, leaving a fiery red streak through the sky. Flying through the crisp, clean air, Amanda wondered if this was what it felt like to be a bird at the North Pole.

When the carriage landed softly on the ground, Amanda was filled with euphoria. She had never experienced anything so magical.

As the sun finally disappeared behind the white blanket of snow at the horizon, Georgia hurried the ladies on to the last stop of their tour—Santa's home and office. They greeted Mrs. Claus, who invited them in and offered them something to eat—"A cookie, perhaps?"

Amanda and Melinda declined as they had already indulged in several chocolate chip cookies at the hotel. Georgia took a cookie, and then she directed Amanda and Melinda to the wooden doorway of Santa's office. After knocking, a voice boomed from behind the closed door, "Come in, come in."

CHAPTER 14

SANTA MEETS THE CONSULTANT

S anta, upon seeing the women enter, quickly put on his red fur jacket over his white T-shirt and suspenders. "Oh, excuse me," he said as he buttoned up his coat. "I thought you were Mrs. Claus. Come in, come in."

Santa Claus stepped out from behind his desk and walked toward the women. "It's good to see you, Melinda," he said as he leaned down to embrace her.

The bear hug left Melinda breathless. "This is Amanda," she said, catching her breath, "the consultant who will be helping us with our strategy."

Santa turned to Amanda and looked her up and down. Underneath her black puffy down jacket, Amanda had on a pair of high boots, blue jeans, and a blue and gray blazer over her T-shirt. As many of the reporters and guests he hosted at the North Pole dressed in suits, Santa was struck by her casualness.

"Nice to meet you," Santa said as he reached his hand toward Amanda.

"It's an enormous pleasure for me," Amanda said, shaking his hand. "Your village is absolutely breathtaking!"

"Yes, it is, isn't it?" Santa said gleefully. And then Santa became very serious, "I worked seven years to get it to this place, and I will not watch it go down!"

Santa grew distant as he thought about the prospect of losing everything he had built. Turning his back to the women, he looked out the window into the village square and watched the elves go about their daily business. "All those elves out there depend on me," he said woefully.

Craning her neck around Santa's large silhouette, Amanda tried to see what Santa was looking at, but she couldn't. Sensing that the encounter wasn't headed in the right direction, Georgia intuitively started to end the meeting, "Well, we know you're busy Santa. We'll leave you alone to your work. Our meeting starts tomorrow morning at nine a.m. We'll see you then." Santa stood silently before the large window that looked out at the empire he had built. Georgia signaled to the two women and ushered them out the door.

Georgia shut the door to the office, and the women managed to exit Santa's home without disturbing Mrs. Claus, who was making a molten chocolate cake in the kitchen. Melinda and Georgia had already walked halfway across the village square before they realized that Amanda was missing. They walked back to the house and found Amanda standing in the foyer with her eyes closed, blissfully breathing in the decadent chocolate smell coming from Mrs. Claus' oven.

Breaking Amanda's trance, Melinda tapped her shoulder and whispered, "It's time to go." When Amanda came to her senses, she scurried after the women as they made their way across town back to the hotel.

CHAPTER 15
WHAT IS A BRAND?

T he next morning, Amanda set up two easels in the boardroom and prepared the room for their work session. On the easel, she placed a pad of Magic Paper, large pieces of paper backed with sticky tape so that the paper could temporary adhere to walls. This way, Amanda could take notes and then place the large pieces of paper on the walls so her participants could keep an inventory of their ideas.

Amanda situated herself at the head of the old oak table, placing her notebook and pen on the table in front of her chair. She arranged notebooks in front of the other seats around the table. In the center of the table, she spread out a dozen mini-Magic Notepads, small square pieces of Magic Paper the size of an elf's hand, as well as colored Magic Markers.

As Amanda set up the room, Mrs. Claus served breakfast on the sideboard next to the old oak table. The smell of freshly baked croissants and hot Italian Roast coffee quickly filled the room.

Ethan arrived first, and after introducing himself to Amanda, he got a cup of coffee and three croissants before sitting in his usual place at the old oak table.

Georgia arrived next and asked Amanda how her night

at the Chocolate Hotel was. "I dreamed of chocolate," she answered with a wide smile.

Looking around at the room, Georgia noticed that Amanda's papers were in front of Santa's seat. "Oh, you can't sit there," she said nervously. "Santa *always* sits there." They both looked at the place at the head of the table.

Concerned that her first encounter with Santa hadn't gone well, Amanda quickly apologized. She moved her belongings to the opposite side of the table, across from Santa's chair. Now, everything was in its correct place.

Simon and Melinda arrived together as they already had an early morning meeting about the financial state of their corporate sponsors. Simon sized up Amanda as Melinda introduced him. "Just so you know," he said as he reached out his hand, "I'm not really a fan of this branding process. It's expensive and unnecessary. The numbers tell us everything."

"Well," said Amanda as she gave Simon a firm handshake. "I'm hoping that our consumers can tell us everything. And I'm hoping that you will see the value of it in the end."

With their plates of food and cups of coffee, the elves took their seats around the table.

Ten minutes late, Santa entered the room hurriedly with rosy cheeks. "I'm sorry, I'm late. I was just at the reindeer barn to bring Blitzer some of Mrs. Claus' reindeer treats. She's pregnant and needs some extra care. I lost track of time." Santa took his usual seat at the table and nodded to Amanda when he had settled in.

Amanda instructed everyone to grab a Magic Notepad from the table as well as a Magic Marker. "I want you to write down for me what you think the Santa Claus brand stands for," she said. The room grew silent.

"What do you mean what it stands for?" asked Ethan, who had already finished one croissant and was working on his second.

"What do you mean by 'brand' exactly?" added Santa, who was not entirely sold on the idea that the Workshop was a brand.

Looking around the table, Amanda saw that the executives looked confused. "I guess we'll have to start from the beginning," she said, taking a deep breath. "Okay. What's a product?"

To Amanda's surprise, they all raised their hands. She had never been in an executive meeting where people raised their hands. Perhaps this was elf etiquette, she thought to herself. She called on Georgia.

"It's an object that is sold to people—to consumers—something that they can use in their lives."

"Good," Amanda lauded. "Now, what is a brand?"

None of the executives raised their hands, except Melinda, who sheepishly held her hand so low that Amanda barely saw it.

"Well, it's a product that you sell to consumers. But it has a name or a symbol that makes it unique from other products. It sort of has a feeling about it."

"Very good!" said Amanda, pleased with Melinda's answer. "So, a brand has an identity that makes it stand apart from other products, something that consumers derive a feeling from—hopefully, a good feeling. Now, why would it be important to think of your product as a brand?"

Except for Melinda, the executives never even considered that Santa Claus could ever be a brand. "Think about the brands that you purchase for yourself," Amanda said, trying to inspire an answer from the elves. "What about those Fifer hats I saw in the Mega Store yesterday? Why do you buy those?" Amanda knew that the elves liked those Fifer hats. The hat section of the Mega Store was one of the busiest departments in the store. "What if I offered you a new hat—the Amanda hat? Would you buy it?"

"Of course not," Simon blurted out. He was offended by Amanda's suggestion but also knew that she was ignorant of the dressing habits of elves and needed to be educated. "Every elf wears a Fifer hat. They are perfectly sized for our small heads. They are made of the softest alpaca wool imported from Chile. And they are astonishingly warm for our cold North Pole winters." He tipped his Fifer hat at Amanda when he finished his monologue.

"Perfect," said Amanda. "So, back to my question, why is it essential for you to think of your product as a brand? What are the benefits of treating your product as a brand?"

When Amanda prompted them to think of the Fifer hats and how the Fifer company benefits from its brand, the team began to brainstorm reasons why brands are valuable. Amanda wrote these on the easel pad.

Importance of a brand:
- Customer loyalty
- Product superiority
- Price premium
- Higher sales and growth potential
- Higher profits leading to higher R&D investment
- Gain value for the company (Trademark)

Amanda stepped back from the list, pleased. The executives were beginning to understand the benefits of branding. Even Simon, who had expressed concerns about the project, appeared to understand why brands are important.

Amanda proceeded to explain the difference between a product and a brand. "Just because a brand has a 'name' that doesn't make it a brand. Every product has a name. But at best, these products offer consumers some sort of utility. On the other hand, true brands have a meaning imbued in them. They evoke, as Melinda mentioned, a feeling."

Amanda explained further, "Take the Fifer hats. Elves would not consider another brand because they have an emotional attachment to the Fifer brand. It is irreplaceable in their hearts and minds. A product offers functional benefits that give value to the consumer. But a brand offers both functional and emotional benefits that impart a special meaning to a core group of consumer advocates. There is little emotional connection to a product, so a consumer will likely switch when a substitute is offered."

"Companies that create a brand can benefit in many ways," Amanda continued, referring back to the list that the executives created. She discussed how brands often offer consumers something better than their competition, which in turn drives consumer loyalty and higher sales. Because it provides product superiority, a brand can command a higher premium in the marketplace. A price premium leads to higher profits, which means more money for the company to invest in research and new product development. And the more value it creates for the consumer, the higher the value it creates for the company in the form of its trademark.

"There are many financial benefits to branding," said Amanda, looking at Simon and smiling, hoping to convince him of the benefits of branding.

Simon wiggled in his seat but stayed silent.

Amanda continued. "Most business people overlook the fact that the trademark is an asset. It's an intangible asset, and the greater the value we can create with our brand, the greater the overall value of the company."

"Branding also allows the company to grow beyond just the products that it currently makes. Because consumers are loyal to brands, they will likely try new products from the brand, and that leads to growth for the company as a whole," she added.

Santa was nodding his head, "I think I understand. We should think about ourselves as a brand because we want people to love us. We want them to be loyal and to believe in us."

"Exactly," said Amanda.

The group sat pondering all this new information about branding. Branding allowed them greater flexibility to grow. And they all agreed that they needed to turn the tides of their misfortune and do just that—grow.

CHAPTER 16
THE MEANING OF THE SANTA CLAUS BRAND

"**S**o now, going back to the question I asked earlier. Can you write down on a Magic Notepad: What does the Santa Claus brand mean? I want just a few words to express what the brand means."

"Is this really necessary?" asked Simon, who had been patient thus far. "I feel like we are wasting our time. We just need to look at our financials and make a decision about how to take the business forward."

"Simon," reprimanded Georgia. "Where are your manners? Amanda is here to help us. We are too emotionally invested. We need an outside perspective and an expert to help guide us."

Simon tapped his pen nervously as he looked at his empty Magic Notepad.

"Look, Simon," said Santa trying to diffuse the situation. "I'm not entirely sure this thing is going to work, but I'm willing to give it a try if it helps us better deliver on our vision."

Simon shook his head.

"I know this is difficult. But please trust me. I promise you this will help the company," said Amanda. "Now, please write down what the Santa Claus brand means."

Amanda gave the executives a few minutes to think about their brand. With Magic Markers, they wrote their statements on square pieces of paper. When they were done, Amanda collected the Magic Notes and stuck them onto the Magic Paper Pad that rested on the easel. They all looked at the board together.

What Does the Santa Brand Mean?
- Spreading joy
- Bringing smiles
- Surprise in the mail
- Presents all year
- Joy around the world

While they agreed that some of the descriptions over-lapped, several phrases were vastly different. Santa became agitated as he read the various statements. "We have always been about spreading joy! Why didn't all of you write that down?" he demanded to know.

The elves looked at each other uncomfortably and waited for someone else to answer Santa's question. Finally, Georgia spoke up, "I know that's what you always say...but given the situation we are in right now—with people re-gifting and donating our gifts—I don't think we are spreading joy. I wrote that we give surprises in the mail. That's what we are fundamentally doing, right? We're giving them surprises, aren't we?"

"I wrote that we are bringing smiles," Melinda added. "The moment people open the mail, they feel joyful, and they smile. Everyone likes getting gifts."

"Unless it's underwear," Georgia blurted out. "That addition was a complete disaster."

"Who wrote 'Joy around the world'?" Santa wanted to know, as this was the sentiment closest to his own.

Ethan, who was polishing off his third croissant, raised his hand. "You always say that we are about bringing joy," he said with his mouth full. He swallowed his food and then continued, "But Georgia and Melinda have a good point. Are we really spreading joy if our consumers don't like our products?"

"Well, they just don't know good taste when they see it!" Santa sulked as he pushed back his seat from the old oak table and sat with his arms crossed.

CHAPTER 17
THROWING CHOCOLATE

A manda, sensing Santa's irritation, moved the conversation along. "Okay, well, it seems we have our work cut out for us. By the end of this project, we need to clearly define what the Santa Claus brand means. Everyone here should be able to say what the Santa brand means, and there will be no disagreement."

Melinda raised her hand. "Is Santa Claus the brand, or is Santa's Workshop the brand?"

Amanda paused for a moment. "I don't know the answer to that question yet. Let's find out from consumers what they have a stronger emotional connection with."

"Consumers? What do you mean?" asked Santa.

"Well, this is a good segue into our next topic." Amanda ripped off a piece of the Magic Paper that had been covered with the executives' Magic Notes about what the brand means and tacked it on the wall so that she could refer to it later if she needed to. Then she wrote in big letters across the clean white sheet of Magic Paper: "Target."

"Now, it's essential for us to understand who our consumer is." She pointed back to the list that they had created on the value of a brand. "We said that we want to have loyal customers and that a brand has meaning to these customers.

Who are our customers?"

"Everybody," they all chimed in together.

"I'm glad we can agree on something!" Santa said, giving out a big laugh.

"Everybody," Amanda thought to herself. She had to remind herself that the people in the room were not all marketers, and she needed to quickly find a way to explain the concept of target marketing. Standing by the easel and deliberating on how best to explain this, Amanda thought of an idea. She went to her handbag and pulled out a bag of chocolate and a wrapped chocolate truffle. Being a choco-holic was useful at times.

Amanda opened the bag of candy-coated, button-shaped chocolate she had bought at a bulk candy store, and poured the colorful candies into her right hand. She stepped back and looked at everyone around the table. And then, with an underhanded pitch, she threw the candies into the air at the executives and yelled, "Catch!"

The candies created a colorful hailstorm in the air. Some of the sweets fell to the ground while others landed on the old oak table and bounced several times before stopping. Like a kid diving into a mound of candy after a piñata explosion, Ethan jumped out of his seat and grabbed three candies that had fallen near him. "I got some candy!" he said with glee.

On the table in front of Santa, there was a single red candy. He popped it into his mouth and let the candy melt into a river of chocolate bliss. A voice broke his concentration. Santa looked up toward the sound, just as the words "Here Santa, catch!" registered in his mind. Santa sat up in his chair and watched as a large golden-wrapped ball of chocolate came toward him in the air. He held out his hands as if playing catcher at a championship baseball game. Santa caught the ball of chocolate and gave out a laugh. "Ho, Ho, Ho, that was a piece of cake—Mrs. Claus' cake!" The executives chuckled with Santa. Since the company had been experiencing problems, Santa didn't joke much, and the elves missed his sense of humor.

"Here is my point," said Amanda. She lifted up the bag of chocolate, which still had a few more candies in it. "You can either send a bunch of messages to everyone, some of whom may not even care about your message, and hope that someone will hear it. Or you can," she pointed to Santa Claus, who was savoring his chocolate truffle, "target someone receptive to your message…get their attention, and then give them something that they really want."

The executive team thought about Amanda's demonstration. Georgia was the first to speak, "You mean if we pick who we want to talk to and really speak to them…we will be able to better meet their needs?"

Amanda nodded her head. The executives chewed on this idea of target marketing as they ate the chocolate that Amanda graciously passed around the table.

CHAPTER 18
TARGET MARKETING FOR SANTA'S WORKSHOP

"**B**ut if we were to pick one target consumer, doesn't that mean that we will lose the revenue of the people we don't target?" Simon asked.

"Yes, that might be so. But if you meet the needs of your target consumer, you are bound to make more money from them in the long run. You've heard the 80/20 rule, right?" Amanda asked.

"Of course. Eighty percent of your profits come from the top twenty percent of your consumers," Simon answered.

"I'm just saying, focus on the twenty percent. It will make the Workshop more efficient in marketing, and it will be more profitable in the long run."

Simon nodded his head. He understood the financial implications of targeting, though he still didn't buy into the whole branding project.

"Let's decide now. Who is your target?" asked Amanda.

"Really, do we have to pick?" Santa asked. "I want to bring joy to everyone."

Already prepared to get resistance from Santa on the topic of targeting, Amanda explained, "I am going to recommend research because we need to understand what drives these consumers. We can find out what our most important consumers believe about the brand. We can also talk to some of your secondary consumers to see if their attitudes are the same or different."

"Research?" Santa seemed baffled by the suggestion.

"Isn't that expensive?" asked Simon.

"Research is the best way we can get into the hearts and minds of our target consumers," said Amanda. "You'll see. It'll be well worth it."

"If I had to be honest, I think our target consumers are children," said Melinda. "That's where we started when we opened seven years ago. And over the years, we expanded to women and men, and they're the ones who aren't satisfied. To my knowledge, we haven't been getting returns from children."

"Well, except for the underwear and socks," added Georgia.

"Kids need underwear and socks," Santa said defensively.

"They need it, but it doesn't necessarily mean that you have to provide it," said Amanda.

"I'm with Melinda. Kids are our target," said Georgia.

"All kids?" asked Amanda. "That's still a big market."

"Maybe not all kids, but definitely kids in elementary school and younger," Georgia answered. "When kids enter middle school, they're not so interested in toys anymore."

"That's an excellent point," Amanda lauded. "We probably want to focus on younger children who enjoy getting toys as gifts. Toys are, after all, a major output of the Workshop."

"But I think it is important to give adults something to be joyful about...they don't get much joy in their everyday lives," implored Santa. "We read the news from around the world. They get up and then sit in traffic for hours to go to their jobs. Sometimes they go to a thankless job. They listen to their bosses drone on and on in a windowless cubicle, or they sit in a factory doing repetitive work, or maybe they do hard manual labor. They need a little joy too!"

"I agree with Amanda and the 80/20 rule. Let's talk to kids. They are our bread and butter. Efficiency. Focus. I like that," Simon argued, still wondering what the research was going to set them back. At least if they narrowed the focus on kids, it would be less expensive than talking to everyone.

Ethan, who had been quiet for some time, added his opinion. "I don't know. Santa has a point. I like to get gifts. I love it when Mrs. Claus gives me her butter pecan cookies. Adults need gifts too."

"And don't forget that we have corporate sponsors," reminded Melinda. "Our sponsors license the Santa Brand, and the funds we get from them underwrite our gifts. They actually make it possible for kids to get gifts at all."

Amanda took inventory of all the targeting challenges that the group raised and then made a list of all the people that it made sense to talk to. On her Magic Paper she wrote down:

Target (for Consumer Research):
- Kids 4–5 years old (preschool)
- Kids 6–8 years old (early elementary school)
- Parents of kids 4–8 years old
- Corporate sponsors

"Okay. I think we should talk to young kids—broken

down into preschool and early elementary school groups," explained Amanda. "We can also talk to their parents to get an adult perspective. This way, we'll know for sure if targeting just kids makes sense or if there is an opportunity with adults. And of course, we need to talk with our corporate sponsors—our bread and butter for Santa's Workshop." She paused to read the room and noticed that Santa's face was puffy and red.

"What's the matter, Santa?" she asked.

"I just think it's sad that we might not include older kids, teenagers, and older adults," Santa said softly.

"Santa, this is very consistent with the omnibus study that we do every year," Melinda said. "The study shows kids under the age of eight are the most positive to Santa Claus, and most adults are neutral to negative about Santa Claus. I don't know why that is, but it is."

"But what about teenagers? They're still kids," Santa sulked.

"Teenagers, according to our omnibus study, are still positive to Santa. But then you have to look at other data. Last year we did a study and asked teens and preteens what they are most interested in. Their top interests are friends, music, clothing, and sports. Santa Claus was 123 on the list."

"123!" Georgia exclaimed as she thought of how much time she spent developing Santa's line of teen products. "We should discontinue the whole teen line!"

"That's the most sensible thing I've heard all day," said Simon joining in.

"That might well be the result of this work. But for now, can we agree that these are the consumers we should talk to?" Amanda said as she referred to the list of people on the board.

"I know we are talking to parents, so that makes me feel good," said Santa. "But I'd still like to understand how teens view the Workshop...and me, for that matter."

"I understand your desire to talk to teens," said Amanda. "When we go into the field, we'll ask to speak with teens in the household when appropriate."

Satisfied with Amanda's concession, Santa nodded his head in agreement.

"What are you going to talk about with these people?" he asked.

Amanda explained that she would travel around the world and interview a select group of consumers within the target groups that they'd identified. She would conduct these interviews in their homes, then report her findings to the team. Ideally, the whole team would be going into the field, but given the business needs, the executives agreed that Melinda would travel with Amanda on behalf of the group.

"You sit with them in their homes?" Simon asked, thinking of how awkward it would be to have strangers come into your home.

"Yes, and you get to see how our consumers live and what's important to them. It's really a remarkable experience," Amanda explained.

Melinda agreed, "I can't wait...it's going to be really exciting!"

The team sat in silence. While the organization received letters and calls from their consumers, they had never undertaken a formal market research project like this. They'd done quantitative studies, but not a qualitative study like this one. Amanda used this as an opportunity to inspire the team. "Trust me, we will learn a lot from these interviews. And the next time we meet, we will decide who will be our target, and we'll design our brand around that target. Does that sound good?"

Though they were very apprehensive, the executives, including Santa, slowly nodded their heads in agreement. While Santa tried to remain calm, his stomach was turning upside down. There was a possibility that the Workshop could be entirely and radically reinvented, and it made him shudder to think that the company he spent years building could be taken into a wholly new direction.

Amanda faced the group and left them with some hopeful words of advice. "It is crucial that we remain true to what Santa Claus has created here. No brand, even brands that need reinvention, should walk entirely away from the equities it has built over the years. We need to honor Santa's vision and make this a stronger brand for the future."

Amanda's speech made an impact on Santa. His cheeks fluttered with a rosy color, and a smile returned to his face.

CHAPTER 19
ASPIRATIONS

Amanda described the next steps of their project. After gathering insights from consumer research, they would then develop a positioning for the brand during a two-day work session. "A positioning, or what I call a brand promise, is a short, concise statement that encapsulates what the brand promises to the consumer and how it is different from other brands. A consumer is bombarded with tons of messages from brands every day, all competing for her attention. A brand based on a single-minded idea that is delivered consistently has a better chance of standing out and reaching her. By the end of this project, we will all be able to articulate what the brand is about. I'll explain more about the tools we use for branding when we meet next."

She looked around the room and saw that the executives were alert and paying attention. "One final thing," Amanda said, "I want you to write on a Magic Notepad what you want as a result of this project. Write down what your hope is for this project. One idea from each of you."

The five executives—Santa, Georgia, Simon, Ethan, and Melinda—took a Magic Notepad and a Magic Marker and got busy writing what they wanted out of the project. Amanda wrote her hope as well. Then, she prepared a clean sheet of Magic Paper on the easel pad.

Amanda collected the pieces of Magic Notes and stuck them onto the Magic Paper under the heading "Project Hopes." The Magic Notes read:

- Strengthen our relationship with our sponsors
- Make kids smile around the world
- Be a joyful company again
- Reinvigorate Santa's vision
- Be a financially healthy company
- Be one of the most talked-about brands in the world

Amanda read these aloud to the group. She was happy to see that everyone had strong ambitions for the project. And she knew that with focus and collaboration, they would be able to accomplish everything on their list. Amanda gave the team her commitment that they would be able to look back at this list at the end of the project and feel that the team was on their way to reaching these goals.

Amanda thanked the executives for their time and then closed the meeting. As she packed up her belongings, she thought about how challenging this project would be. The group was open to changes, but Santa, who was very wedded to his own ideas about the brand, was resistant. But Amanda was confident about one thing—the consumers would help her identify the growth opportunities for Santa's Workshop. She was excited to learn what the corporate sponsors and the children had to say about Santa.

CHAPTER 20
THE SPONSORS

Melinda gave Amanda a list of Santa's Workshop's corporate sponsors and an overview of their businesses. Amanda immediately saw that most of the companies were consumer brands targeted to kids and families—mainly companies that produced juice drinks, food, and soft goods like clothing, backpacks, and bedding. They all used Santa's image on the products they manufactured and marketed around the world. Amanda made appointments to meet with four of the top corporate sponsors immediately.

Her meetings with the sponsors were illuminating. She learned that the sponsors really liked Santa's mission to spread joy to children. They liked the idea of giving unconditionally, as it was easy to understand. Many of the sponsors began licensing Santa's image within the first two years of operations and started to put Santa on their products year-round. They loved his focus on children because their products were targeted toward children or mothers with children. The companies' relationships with Santa's Workshop has paid off. Following the licensing and distribution of their Santa-inspired products, their sales took off immediately.

The sponsors talked excitedly to Amanda about their products. The representative from the food manufacturer gave her a tour of the company, and she met all the brand managers and food scientists who developed the line of Santa's products. She had a product sampling of the juices from the beverage manufacturer and sat in on an advertising pitch from their agency for their upcoming television campaign. The home goods licensee took her to the largest store of their most significant retail account and showed her all the products merchandised in a special Santa's Workshop section. And the kid's clothing manufacturer showed Amanda their designer studio where the initial designs for the clothing were conceived and developed.

The sponsors were proud of their products, and they were very dedicated to serving their consumers—kids. One thing that became clear in the interviews was that the key to aligning with the interests of the sponsors was refocusing the Workshop's efforts on targeting kids. The key to making the sponsors happy was to make kids happy.

In their first few years of producing Santa items, these companies experienced double-digit growth due to the popularity of Santa and his Workshop. They were thrilled to be affiliated with such a strong symbol of altruism and goodness. But over the last two years, they felt that the Workshop had lost its way, and their sales of Santa items had softened. This year has been the worst yet, with sales projected to be flat or negative for the first time since their licensing agreements with Santa's Workshop began. This was most disconcerting to the sponsors, as they all feared that it was the beginning of an unfortunate trend.

But sales were only part of what concerned them about their sponsorship with Santa, as Amanda found out in her interviews.

"I heard that Santa is running a sweatshop at the North Pole," said the juice licensee. "I had to call Melinda to find out if it was true. She assured me that it wasn't, but I want to know for sure."

The food manufacturer had heard the same rumors, and he hoped the reindeer and elves were being treated fairly. "We have an extensive line of food that features Santa's elves and reindeer, like our Leaven Elf Breads and Reindeer Crunch Cereal. Our consumers would be irate if these rumors were true."

"I see men wearing those hideous ties," said the kids' clothing licensee. "I really have to question Santa's tastes… really now."

"Someone told me that the Workshop was thinking of making boats and motorcycles," said their home goods licensee. This caught Amanda by surprise, as she wasn't aware of any plans for developing these types of products. But, knowing Santa and his new product development frenzy, she didn't doubt the veracity of the rumor. "Well," the sponsor went on to say, "if that is the case, we might have to reconsider our relationship with Santa. Our company stands for quality and affordability in simple, everyday home items like sheets and towels. Boats and motorcycles are way too extravagant. This is not the kind of message we want to send to our consumers."

Amanda continued to ask this select group of corporate sponsors many questions about their perceptions of Santa and their experience with the Workshop. They reiterated their belief in Santa's initial strategy of bringing joy to kids. In fact, that's why they all became sponsors. But now they universally felt that Santa had diluted his message by expanding his line of products. Finally, Amanda asked them about their thoughts about the future of Santa's Workshop. They all expressed concern that they might have to sever their sponsorship arrangement with Santa's Workshop if things didn't improve. But they assured Amanda that they would do everything they could to help turn around the Workshop.

With her new knowledge about the sponsors' interests, Amanda was ready to take on the next phase of the research plan—talking to kids around the world. She had arranged to meet with thirty kids and their parents in six different countries—the United States, Mexico, France, India, China, and South Africa. While she was excited to get started, she also felt apprehensive. After all, going "into the field," as researchers called it, required a small leap of faith. There were many unknown factors that she might encounter. But still, she couldn't wait to start interviewing children to uncover the truth about Santa and his brand.

CHAPTER 21
TURMOIL AT THE WORKSHOP

At Santa's Workshop, things had gone from bad to worse in the weeks following the "Snowball Incident," as it had been dubbed by the North Pole News. Santa quelled the elves' anxiety over the future of the Workshop for a little while, but the elves were still frustrated and overworked. As a result, their work suffered, and productivity at the Workshop plummeted even further. According to Aidan, even the reindeer acted strangely sluggish and moody. For the first time, the reindeer began fighting over the food they shared, even though they always had plenty to eat.

Because productivity had fallen so precipitously, the executives had to come up with a plan to make two hundred more gifts that month. Though they knew it would make them very unpopular, they suggested to Santa that they ask the elves to stay an extra half-hour on their shifts. Santa agreed to the plan, but he worried about how it would affect the already fragile state of the Workshop.

When Ethan delivered the news to the elves on the day shift, the elves became irate and refused to put in any more hours. At their usual quitting time, all of the elves walked out. This shocked the executives. They thought the elves would do everything they could to make sure the kids got their gifts. The executives were even working on the toy lines for five to six hours a day just to make up for gaps in production.

"But I don't understand," said Santa, after Ethan shared the news that the elves refused to work longer hours. "I thought they understood that things were going to turn around. Everyone has to do their part."

"They understand…but nothing has changed yet," said Ethan. He knew the plan to increase the elves' hours was a bad idea. "They are already overworked, and to ask them to work even more is adding insult to injury. They are very anxious about this branding project."

"You all made me promise to give this branding thing a chance. I'll give Amanda a call and see if they can do the interviews faster."

"Amanda said they have a pretty strict schedule to keep. I doubt they'll be able to change it this late in the game." Ethan paused, and then tentatively asked, "Can't we make a decision now to cut production of some of our lines? You heard Melinda—teenagers don't even believe in Santa. Let's stop making items for them. Or how about we cut production of the underwear and socks? We all know that it isn't really aligned with bringing joy to people."

Santa sat back in his chair. He had built the company and shutting down a part of his company was like shutting down a part of himself. "Can't we just wait another three weeks? Amanda and Melinda will be back, and we'll have a better idea of what to do after we get all the information."

Ethan knew in his heart that three weeks was too long.

But he didn't want to argue with Santa. Santa, once the eternal optimist, looked stressed and tired, and Ethan could tell that the problems at the Workshop were starting to take a toll on him. Ethan reluctantly nodded his head in agreement and then left Santa's office in silence.

CHAPTER 22
TOMMY AND BETTY

Amanda and Melinda arrived at their first home in Hackensack, New Jersey—a white colonial house with green shutters. The women followed the path of slate rocks leading to the front door. Amanda resolutely walked up to the door and rang the doorbell while Melinda approached the door tentatively, noticing the 'Welcome to the Johnsons' placard in the landscaped garden adjacent to the doorway.

Betty answered the door, and shortly after opening it, Tommy popped his head in the doorway.

"I've been expecting you," said Betty. "Tommy is excited that we are having guests." She introduced herself and her son to the ladies and then invited the women to come in to sit down in the living room.

Amanda and Melinda made their way through the landmine of toys covering the beige wall-to-wall carpeting in the living room. When they made it safely to the couch in the far corner of the room, Amanda gave Betty and Tommy an overview of the interviews. She explained that she worked for an independent research company that talks to people about all kinds of things—from coffee to cars to Santa Claus—which was what they were going to talk about today.

"I love Santa Claus!" said Tommy. Betty told Tommy to quiet down so the ladies could talk.

Amanda explained that they would be interviewing Tommy first, and then they'd talk to Betty. Amanda relayed the importance of being open and honest, as all the information that they received was intended to help improve their services to people like them.

Tommy jumped on the couch as Amanda got comfortable next to him. Betty sat next to Tommy on the other side of the sofa. Melinda took a seat in an armchair in the corner of the room so she could watch from a distance and take notes.

"Tommy, can you tell me how old you are?" Amanda asked.

"Four," he said, sticking up four fingers on his right hand.

"And what is your favorite thing to do?"

"Playing with my toys."

"Who is Santa?"

"A big man."

"Big man?" Amanda wanted clarification.

"Who lives in the North Pole," he said.

"And what does he do?"

Tommy's forehead wrinkled as he pondered the question. After a long pause, he shouted, "He gives gifts!" He jumped up from his seat and yelled behind him, "He got me a truck!" Tommy ran into the next room and came back with a big yellow truck.

"He loves that truck. He got it in the mail from Santa three months ago," Betty explained. "He won't put the thing away. He slept with it for several days when he first got it.

And then I convinced him that George, his stuffed animal, missed sleeping with him."

"Vvvvrrrooooommm," Tommy sang as he knelt on the ground and pushed the truck across the beige carpeting.

"Tommy," Amanda said. "How did you feel when you got a package from Santa?"

Tommy looked up from his truck. "Happy."

Betty elaborated on Tommy's answer, "He wasn't just happy. He was elated. He said, 'Wow!' at least five times." Amanda nodded as she listened to Betty. Melinda kept quiet to allow Amanda to establish rapport with Tommy and his mom.

"Tommy, can you tell me what you did when you got the package?" Amanda asked.

As Tommy drove the truck backwards, he started to make a beeping noise.

"Tommy," his mother cautioned, "answer the lady's question."

He looked up from his truck as he sat squatting on the floor. "It was kind of hard to open. My mom had to help. We got it open and this was in it!" Tommy jumped like a frog off the ground as a smile ran across his face.

Melinda sat quietly taking notes. As Amanda had instructed her, she paid particular attention to the respondents' behavior, as well as his speech. She made a note of Tommy's excitement as he spoke about his gift from Santa.

Amanda asked, "Why do you think Santa sent you this gift?"

As he continued to rock back and forth, Tommy looked up at Amanda and shrugged his shoulders. Then he went back to dragging his truck across the floor.

"Tommy, answer the lady's question," Betty said again.

Without looking up from his toy, he said, "Because he likes kids."

"Is there anything else?" Amanda asked. Tommy continued playing with his truck. "Tommy?" she said, trying to get his attention.

"I don't know. He wants people to be happy?" Tommy moved his truck to the far corner of the room.

"Tommy, come here when the lady is talking to you," Betty said to her son. "I'm sorry…he's a very active boy. He really loves that truck. Sometimes I can't get him to stop playing with it."

"It's okay," Amanda said, "I can ask you a few questions as he plays." Amanda watched Tommy move the truck in a circle around his body as he made the sound, "Vvvvrroooooommmm."

CHAPTER 23
A SCARF TO BE FORGOTTEN

Amanda shifted her attention back to Betty. "I'll ask you some of the same questions I asked Tommy, and a few more. Is that okay?"

Betty shook her head, "That shouldn't be too difficult then."

"Who is Santa?"

"His real name is Nicholas, I think. He moved to the North Pole and started a toy company for kids. He says his mission is to spread joy. Oh, and he works with elves."

"What is your overall impression of him?"

"Santa? Oh, I don't know. He's jolly and…happy. He's got a good attitude about life. He's generous. He likes kids."

"How is he generous?" Amanda asks.

"Well, he gives all these gifts to people. Not just kids… but I got a gift too. Gifts are great."

"What makes a gift so great?" Amanda asked.

"Oh, I don't know. It makes you feel special. It says, 'I've been thinking about you.' It feels good to get a gift." She said with a smile. But as she thought about it more, the smile left her face. "Except, Santa's last gift…well…"

Amanda sensed Betty's reluctance to continue. "Please," Amanda said, "You're not going to hurt my feelings. I want you to be as open and honest as possible."

She hesitated, then continued, "Well, he sent me a gift too. It was a scarf. And it wasn't really my style."

"What did you do with it?"

"I gave it to my mother," Betty admitted. "I guess Santa got it wrong. He knew exactly what Tommy wanted. Well, Tommy wrote to him and asked specifically for the truck. But he had no clue about me. I didn't expect anything. I guess I thought it was kind of wasteful that he sent me a gift."

Melinda looked up from her notebook. "You found it wasteful?" she asked. As Melinda's voice rang out, the two women turned their heads to the corner of the room.

Betty looked at Melinda, "Don't get me wrong...it's awesome getting a gift when you least expect it. But it makes you think that a person didn't really think about it when you get something you don't want. So, then what's the point of getting a gift? Do you know what I mean?" Amanda and Melinda nodded as Betty rambled on.

"Then I thought that Santa was just being opportunistic—that he was just playing lip service to this whole 'joy' thing. I don't know...maybe I'm a little jaded. What is this guy trying to do? What makes him the expert on this happiness thing?" Betty looked worried, "Oh, you probably didn't want to hear that, did you?"

"No. We did. Like I said, there are no right or wrong answers," Amanda said. "What about Tommy? Do you think he thinks the same way as you?"

"Oh, my gosh, no! He loves that truck. He talks about Santa like he's some kind of magical wizard. I mean...Santa has elves. I personally don't believe in that kind of stuff. I've never seen an elf. As far as I'm concerned, they don't exist." She looked at Melinda and smiled.

Melinda looked more like a very short person than an elf, so Betty had little reason to believe that she was offending her. Betty leaned toward Amanda and Melinda, then whispered to the women so that Tommy couldn't hear. "Tommy believes in fairies and dragons."

In the far end of the living room by the windows, Tommy was whirling the truck around in a figure eight on the floor, completely absorbed in his playtime.

CHAPTER 24
TRUCKS CAN'T FLY

Amanda got up from her seat and walked over to the window where Tommy was playing, carefully avoiding the drum set and train set that was in her path. The sunlight created shadow box lines on the carpeting through the windows panes, which by habit, she also avoided.

"Tommy," she said as she got on her hands and knees. "Tell me more about Santa. What do you know about him?"

"He has a big laugh. I heard it once on the television," he said as he moved his truck backward and forward on the floor.

"What else?"

"He has reindeer…they fly!" he said with a gleam in his eyes. "I'd like to see that!"

"What's so interesting about that?" Amanda asked casually.

"Flying reindeer. Come on…" said Tommy, looking at her like she was ridiculous. "Reindeer are totally cool!"

"Oh…I forgot about the flying reindeer!" Betty said from across the room, trying not to sound sarcastic.

Amanda sensed the doubt in Betty's voice. It took every ounce of restraint not to jump up and say, "But they are real. I saw them with my own eyes! They are magnificent creatures, and I got to fly in a carriage pulled by reindeer!" Instead, she turned to Tommy and nonchalantly said, "Yeah…they're cool."

"And elves. They help Santa. They're little people…just like me!" he said excitedly.

"What do you know about elves?"

"Elves work in a workshop. They made this…with their own hands!" Tommy lifted up the toy into the air. "Look… my truck can fly just like the reindeer!" Skillfully avoiding the toys on the ground, he ran around the room, using both of his hands to glide the big yellow truck in the air.

Amanda looked at Melinda, and they both smiled with amusement at Tommy. "Be careful, Tommy!" his mother yelled as he got dangerously close to her china cabinet filled with Hummel figurines. As she watched the yellow truck fly in the air, she shouted, "Tommy, put that thing down! Trucks can't fly!"

Tommy continued to play as if the adults were invisible. Melinda leaned over and whispered, "I think it's one of those special flying trucks from Santa's Workshop."

Betty gave Melinda a weak smile and turned her attention back to Amanda, who was sitting across the room. "Now, where were we?"

CHAPTER 25
ANOTHER FIGHT

While Amanda and Melinda traveled around the world to complete their research project, more trouble began to brew at the North Pole. The atmosphere at the cantina was always festive; after all, the elves loved eating more than anything in the world—after making toys, that is. It was a place where the elves could enjoy good times with their fellow elves and eat delectable food cooked by Chef Aaron. But since the Snowball Incident, the atmosphere of the cantina was somber at best.

It used to be that the elves picked up their food in the commissary line and then walked into the dining hall to find an empty seat. They sat wherever there was space. But after the problems at the Workshop began, the elves started sitting with their work teams. The toymakers sat with the toymakers. The makers of sporting goods sat with the makers of sporting goods. And the sock and underwear makers sat with other garment makers. And the two perfume makers, the newest to arrive at the North Pole, always sat together—alone in the far corner.

As of late, there were rumors that the socks and underwear lines would be discontinued. The toymakers found this rather amusing and began to make fun of the sock and underwear makers. During the lunchtime rush, Toymaker Christopher, who sat at a table with other toymakers, watched as Kimberly walked through the dining hall toward a table where her fellow sock makers were eating.

"Socks are for sissies!" yelled Christopher as Kimberly passed his table.

Kimberly stopped in her tracks. "Socks keep you warm. What do toys do?" she retorted defensively.

"Toys make you happy!" Christopher exclaimed.

"Toys break!"

"Socks get holes!"

The toymakers and the garment makers listened to Christopher and Kimberly's banter. Then a banana flew through the air and fell to the ground right in front of Kimberly's feet. Irate, Kimberly put her tray down on Christopher's table, picked up her bowl of spaghetti, and dumped it onto his head. He got up from his seat and threw his glass of milk on her shirt.

Soon, food was being thrown around from every which way. Corn. Mashed potatoes. Chicken. Popcorn. Ice cream cones. Everything on the menu was jettisoned into the air. Soon, the volleys, which started between the toymakers and the sock makers, became a free-for-all between doll makers, tie makers, and every other kind of maker.

Ethan, who was in the cantina at the time, tried to stop the food fight, but he got a pie thrown in his face for his efforts. He wiped the blueberry off his face, licked his lips and fingers, and then ran to get Santa in his office.

When Santa arrived at the cantina, the entire room was covered with food. Santa stood in shock as he assessed the state of the room. "What is going on here?" he bellowed. His usually jolly demeanor had turned sour. "Who started this fight?" The food fight slowly stopped.

Standing in the wake of the food fight was Chef Aaron, the most renowned chef in all of Elfland. "I cannot work like this, Santa. I am this close to quitting!" he yelled with his thumb and his forefinger held up high as if he were holding up a pea.

The whole room gasped in shock as Chef Aaron uttered his angry words. The departure of Chef Aaron would be a devastating loss to the North Pole.

Chief Toymaker Jacob, a brave soul, stood up and spoke: "Santa, everyone is afraid they are going to lose their jobs. And there are rumors that we are shutting down. Are we closing down?"

Suddenly Santa understood that the "repositioning" of the brand could have unpopular consequences for the elves. "Let's be clear here. We are not going out of business. We're going to turn this around. Even if we have to make the difficult decision to stop production of some of our lines, we'll retrain elves to work in other parts of the workshop. We are a family. We will always be a family."

A hum of conversation swept across the lunchroom. Just then, Simon and Georgia arrived. With gaping mouths, they simultaneously uttered, "Oh my!"

Santa assured Chef Aaron that his food would never be thrown like that again, and then asked the elves to pick up the food that had fallen on the ground and onto the tables. The cafeteria aides came out from behind the commissary line with brooms and dustpans and began sweeping up the mess.

Simon and Georgia stood with Santa and watched the elves slowly clean the cantina. Santa crossed his arms and admitted to his executives that he was grateful that Amanda and Melinda would be returning that evening. Before leaving, Santa said one last thing to Simon and Georgia in sotto voce. He said, "We'll bring love back into this place."

As Santa turned to leave the lunchroom, he slipped on a slice of tiramisu that was in his path. With nimble arms, Simon and Georgia caught him just in time to avert a fall.

CHAPTER 26
TIME TO CLEAN UP

The elves on the afternoon shift went back to work, where they were met with lectures by their supervisors about the food fight. The others returned to the Castle to relax for the rest of the day. The town was quiet, except for the sounds of the brisk summer winds.

When Melinda and Amanda arrived at the North Pole after their long trip, there was little indication of the turmoil facing the Workshop. But as soon as they arrived at the cantina to grab an early dinner, they discovered that all, in fact, was not well. The cafeteria aides were still cleaning up what was left of the lunchtime food fight. Noodles hung from the ceiling like streamers at a holiday party, and applesauce clung to the walls like Silly Putty. While watching one lunch aide stand on a ladder to clean the ceiling, Amanda uttered, "Looks like we arrived just in time."

Amanda and Melinda selected their food from the cafeteria line, then retreated to a table in the corner of the room with their trays. Lost in thought about the two days in front of them, they enjoyed their dinner of turkey and gravy, mashed potatoes, and apple pie in silence. They had so much information that they wanted to share about the research they had conducted. Amanda remembered their first kick-off meeting two months ago when none of the executives could agree on what the Santa brand means. She knew that she was going to have a tough job getting the executives aligned on a new strategy for the Santa Claus brand.

As Amanda and Melinda finished dinner, the aides finished cleaning the cafeteria, wiping clean any evidence of a food fight. The aides returned to their spots on the cantina line to help with the dinner service. The dinner rush was just beginning when Amanda and Melinda retired to their rooms at the Chocolate Hotel.

With comfort food filling her belly, Amanda settled into her room and spent a few hours preparing for their meeting the next day. She turned out the light at eleven o'clock to ensure that she had enough sleep before the meeting, which she knew would be both exciting and taxing. As she fell asleep, she dreamed about flying in a sleigh pulled by twelve reindeer high above the North Pole. She was sitting next to Santa, who was steering the sleigh and laughing, "Ho, ho, ho!"

CHAPTER 27
A NEW PERSPECTIVE

Amanda woke up to an already bright July day. She felt refreshed and ready to challenge the team to create the new Santa's Workshop. Like last time, Amanda arrived early to set up the boardroom for their two-day work session. She set up her easels with fresh pads of Magic Paper and made sure she had enough multi-colored Magic Markers and Magic Notepads for the team members. She also placed a few small toys made by the elves on the table. The toys provided some much-needed mental stimulation during the long sessions, and they reminded the participants of all the wonderful products that were created at the Workshop.

As Amanda got ready for the session, Mrs. Claus arrived to set up breakfast, greeting Amanda with a smile as she placed an urn filled with freshly brewed coffee onto the sideboard next to the old oak table. She set up cups, milk, and sugar, and placed a platter filled with warm homemade blueberry muffins and raspberry scones next to the coffee urn. Then Mrs. Claus left to start making lunch for the group.

The executives began to arrive one by one. Georgia carried a large file full of marketing plans and innovation ideas. She came prepared with her thoughts on how to simplify production. Simon had a file folder containing the Workshop's current budget and financial forecasts. He placed the papers and his notepad on the table in front of him and then lined up his pocket calculator precisely one inch to the left of his notepad. Having taken copious notes in the field with Amanda, Melinda had her notebook filled with quotes and ideas on how to improve the Workshop. Ethan brought a healthy appetite; he picked up two blueberry muffins from the breakfast buffet, poured himself a large cup of coffee, and then sat down.

Though punctual, Santa arrived last. He was working in his office when Mrs. Claus reminded him that everyone was getting settled for the meeting. Santa said hello to everyone and then sat down at his usual spot at the head of the old oak table. Amanda offered him a cup of coffee, but he turned it down as he already had three cups that morning. Amanda hoped that his visible anxiety was a result of the caffeine, not his nervousness over the project.

As Amanda stood in front of the executives, she noticed that they all looked tired. Santa Claus had called Amanda while she was in the field and encouraged her to come back to the North Pole as quickly as possible. Unfortunately, having committed to their research plan, they could not shorten their trip. She knew that the situation at the Workshop was not good, as evidenced by the remnants of the food fight last night. She knew that she had only one shot to help the Workshop. Her heart started to drum loudly as she began to feel the pressure of the project weighing on her. But then she remembered her dream of flying in the air with Santa Claus.

Amanda took a deep breath, and a thought came to her.

"We need to mix things up," she said to the executives. "Let's all take different seats today. This day is about challenging what we know and doing things differently. That means I need you to get out of your element. Switch seats. Do it quickly."

Simon, Melinda, Ethan, and Georgia exchanged glances, dreading the repercussions of Amanda's request. Santa got up first and said, "I like the way you think, Amanda! Get up, everyone. Let's switch seats."

Santa moved two seats to his right, to Melinda's place. Simon moved to Georgia's chair, Melinda to Simon's, and Georgia to Ethan's. Ethan was left to take Santa's seat. He sank gingerly into the large leather seat, still warm from Santa's body, and gave Santa an awkward grin. He had brought his two blueberry muffins with him and began eating quietly, trying to avoid any eye contact with his colleagues.

CHAPTER 28
CONSUMER PROFILES

The first thing that Amanda wanted to do was to tell the executives everything she and Melinda learned from the research they conducted. She took them through an overview of her interviews with the corporate sponsors. Then, she dove into their consumer research learnings.

To bring their consumers to life, Amanda had created large posters, which she leaned against the wall. Each poster prominently featured a photo of a child and a summary of their attitudes about Santa.

"Now, I'm not going to take you through what every child said, but I want to give you a flavor for the types of kids that we met. Let's meet six of these remarkable children," said Amanda.

MEET TOMMY
Age: 4
Lives in: New Jersey, USA
What he likes to do: play with his truck and make it fly
The best thing about being a kid: playing outside and getting dirty

Santa is: a jolly man with flying reindeer
What he likes about getting gifts: unwrapping the present and finding out what it is
His mother: thinks reindeer and trucks can't fly

MEET ANNIKA

Age: 5
Lives in: small village outside of Cape Town, South Africa
What she likes to do: play with 'found' objects like nuts, rubber bands, household items
The best thing about being a kid: getting to hear interesting stories from her grandmother
Santa is: a man with magical powers who sends gifts to people who need them
What she likes about getting gifts: makes her feel special and happy
Her mother: doesn't understand why Santa gives gifts—there must be a catch

MEET ZHANG WEI

Age: 6
Lives in: Beijing, China
What he likes to do: fly his kite in the park high in the sky
The best thing about being a kid: playing and not having to work in a factory, like his parents
Santa is: a man who wears red, like the Chinese flag, and laughs a lot
What he likes about getting gifts: playing with them

right away

His mother: thinks that education is the most important thing and she would rather him study than play

MEET CLAUDETTE

Age: 7

Lives in: Aix-en-Provence, France

What she likes to do: play on the swing set and climb the monkey bars

The best thing about being a kid: dreaming about becoming an astronaut

Santa is: awesome because she got an awesome rocket ship

What she likes about getting gifts: the gifts are really cool, and they're always what she asks for

Her father: wants Claudette to be a doctor because being an astronaut is a pipe dream

MEET JORGE

Age: 8

Lives in: Mexico City, Mexico

What he likes to do: Soccer, soccer, soccer

The best thing about being a kid: making a goooaallll and going to local soccer games with his father

What he thinks of Santa: he is a saint of some sort

What he likes about getting gifts: being surprised

His father: wonders why the gifts he gets from Santa are off the mark, while the ones his kid gets are so much better

MEET SRI

Age: 5

Lives in: Delhi, India

What she likes to do: draw princesses in palaces and play with her doll

The best thing about being a kid: dressing up in her mother's saris and playing make-believe with her sister

What she thinks of Santa: he is funny and has a big laugh

What she likes about getting gifts: unwrapping a present and wishing for a fun toy or dress for her doll

Her mother: wishes that Sri has all the opportunities she didn't have and wants her to get an education and a good-paying job

After introducing these kids to Santa and the other executives, Amanda continued to explain that each of the children grew up in different cultural contexts and socio-economic conditions. But what they all had in common was their love of play. They found ways, whether or not they had fancy toys or found objects, to engage themselves in the activity of play. She said, "Play occurs either with an object or it happens entirely in one's imagination. It is the part of the day that brings enjoyment to a child."

The executives nodded with agreement. They knew that kids love playing because they were once elf kids too. They remembered long days running in the snow or playing on their sleds. Even when they were stuck inside because of bad weather, they played with buttons, marbles, toy train sets, and dolls. Sometimes they sat in a circle and played, "Oaf,

Oaf, Elf," a game similar to the American game of "Duck, Duck, Goose." They even made up stories and put on elaborate plays complete with costumes and scripts. They seemed to have forgotten how important play was to a child.

Amanda went on to say how joyful it was to receive a toy from Santa. Their parents universally agreed that Santa's toys were high quality and that the toys were thoughtfully created with their kids in mind. Kids loved getting toys from Santa and talked about how exciting it was to get a present as a surprise. In other words, the anticipation of getting a gift was fun. Furthermore, opening the package was a special moment. Their mothers or fathers recalled their children jumping up and down, frantically ripping the brown paper off as they opened the gifts. The kids felt special when they received something that they requested.

"Ho, Ho, Ho," said Santa. "I'm glad the kids like our toys. A lot of time and effort goes into making sure those toys are remarkable."

The news was good for the Workshop and their toy line, and everyone felt good about being able to fulfill these kids' wishes. But they couldn't rest on their laurels because there were a few things that Amanda needed to make sure the executives knew, and some of it was not going to be easy to hear.

CHAPTER 29
KIDS VS. ADULTS

"Kids indeed love getting the gifts," Amanda said, continuing with her debrief. "But their parents had a very different perspective about Santa and his motivations. First, many of the parents, like Jorge's father and Tommy's mother, were disappointed with the gifts they personally received, particularly because their kids got something they wanted. Second, they were skeptical of Santa's motivation. They were leery of anyone who wanted to spread joy without wanting anything in return. Basically, adults are cynical about Santa and the Workshop."

There were grunts around the table. "But how could that be," said Santa. "They see how much we make their kids happy."

"They do. Adults know that the gifts bring their kids joy, so they are positive about Santa and the Workshop. But you also have to understand the difference between kids and adults," Amanda explained. "Kids are filled with promise and innocence. Adults are realists, which makes them question anything that is not rational—like elves and flying reindeer. Adults have simply forgotten the idea of play. If you give kids a bag of rocks as a gift, they would be completely mesmerized by the shape of each rock, the color, the composition, the weight, and the texture. They'd find a way to have fun with the rocks. They'd throw them into a lake and study how they went 'kerplunk' in the water, or they'd build something with them like an igloo or a stone garden. But, if you give adults the same bag of rocks as a gift, they'd look at you as if they'd been duped. They'd probably even be insulted."

"How could these adults not believe in elves and flying reindeer?" Santa asked innocently. Although Santa was an adult, he viewed the world entirely from a child's perspective.

"They look at the world very differently Santa, and this shows up in so many facets of their worlds. Kids love to play, to interact, and to pretend. And adults, they work a lot, and if they are not working, they are unwinding. There is hardly time for them to play. But these adults are also our gatekeepers, so we need to make sure we get them to believe that we are doing good for their child."

"I think we could have guessed what adults thought about Santa without spending so much on this research," said Simon.

"I think it was good to get confirmation in the field about how adults feel," said Amanda. "But what we were really after were insights about our kids."

Deep down, Simon knew that the research they did with kids was really insightful, but he was still worried about whether all of this work would lead them to a better financial outcome for the Workshop.

"Did any adults like our gifts?" asked Georgia.

"As a matter of fact, there were a few that did like their gifts—I remember one man in a town outside of Cape Town who liked his new tie and a woman in New Jersey who liked her new wallet. But most of the adults we spoke to either re-gifted or donated their gifts, which confirms the rumors we heard."

The elves looked at each other with raised eyebrows. No one wanted to say it, but they knew that targeting adults was a bad idea.

Santa sat back in his chair and took in the disturbing news. Finally, after a long silence, he asked Amanda, "Are you suggesting that we stop making products for adults?"

"I'm saying that if you want to grow, forget being everything to everyone. Become the best at fulfilling kids' needs," said Amanda.

CHAPTER 30
WHAT ABOUT TEENS?

"**S**o, if we are talking about kids, teens are included, right?" asked Santa.

Amanda reminded Santa of the omnibus study on teens that Melinda had shared with the team during their first meeting. That report had indicated that teens have lost interest in Santa. When Amanda went into the field, she tried to find out if this was true.

As she had promised Santa, Amanda spoke to any teens living in the homes they visited. If they weren't home, she asked the parents about their teenage kids.

The in-home research confirmed the findings in that initial quantitative report—teenagers have lost interest in Santa. They were more concerned with friends, music, sports, and fashion.

"By the time kids are teenagers, Santa is no longer relevant," Amanda said boldly.

The executives gasped at Amanda's statement. While a little harsh, Amanda knew that she had to tell them the truth. Otherwise, they might still believe that it was worthwhile to continue making products for teens.

"No longer relevant," Santa repeated under his breath. He knew that his mission was relevant to the many kids around the world, but it was hard to hear that teens did not appreciate his generosity.

CHAPTER 31
KIDS AND THEIR IMAGINATION

"**T**his brings me to another significant distinction about kids: they live in their imagination. They believe in unicorns, fairies, dragons, and they believe the world can be a better place. And that's why they believe in Santa Claus." Amanda looked around the table. She was pleased that everyone was alert and hanging onto her every word.

"They live in their imagination? I never thought about kids in that way," Georgia said.

Melinda jumped in. "That kid, Tommy from New Jersey, had a great imagination. He liked to fly his truck, and his mom kept telling him that trucks don't fly."

"That's right. I'm glad you brought that up, Melinda. At some point, people lose their ability to imagine and to believe. The kids we talked to have a strong belief in Santa. But when they grow older, they 'learn' that Santa doesn't exist."

"Who is spreading such lies?" Santa demanded to know.

"The few older kids we spoke to said that they learned this from their parents or their friends," Amanda replied. "But along with this, kids slowly lose their ability to imagine and conceive what's possible. They lose faith and start becoming more like adults."

The executives fell silent. To lose faith in something so magical felt depressing to them.

"What Amanda is saying is right," Melinda said. "I think we need to focus on kids four to eight years old. This target was our initial hypothesis for our research, and it's very true. Preteens and teens don't care about Santa anymore. And parents are too jaded. We still need to appeal to them as gatekeepers, but they should not be our primary target."

"So, according to the 80/20 rule you talked about last time, we should focus on these younger kids?" Santa asked.

Pleased that Santa had internalized her arguments about targeting, Amanda nodded her head. "Yes. But we must fulfill their needs with the right products."

"What do you mean by that?" asked Georgia, who started to get nervous that she would have to start developing a new line of products.

"Well, kids love toys because they love to play, and that's what Santa's Workshop should make," Amanda said. She explained further, "One parent said that his son, Bobby, got a pair of underwear two years ago. The kid cried all day long because he was so disappointed. What he wanted was a train set."

Santa's heart sank. Amanda's news was the most upsetting thing he had heard that day. It was far more hurtful than learning that adults and teens didn't appreciate his gifts. He loved children so much, and he wanted to bring them joy, but instead, he had brought a little boy to tears.

"Listen, I know this is difficult to hear," Amanda said, "but let's use this as an opportunity to commit to developing the best and most appropriate products for kids."

A heavy silence fell over the room like a deep blanket of snow.

"So, now what?" said Santa quietly.

"Focus on being the best damn toymaker in the world and delight these kids to the best of your ability," Amanda said passionately, hoping she didn't offend any of the executives when she used the word 'damn.'

The executives were glad that Amanda said what they were all thinking. Georgia wanted so badly to say, "I told you so," but she refrained. Simon could appreciate the bottom line; the company would be more profitable by focusing its efforts on making toys for kids. Ethan loved toys and was thrilled to rally the employees around making toys. He remembered when the Workshop focused solely on toys; the elves were very happy. Thinking about their corporate sponsors, Melinda knew that focusing on kids would make them extremely happy as well.

"So, we'll focus on kids," Santa said. "But, now what?"

"Well, we have to start at the beginning, and that is with the consumer."

CHAPTER 32
TARGETING KIDS

"**N**ow, I explained the concept of target marketing to you last time. Does everyone remember that?" Amanda asked the group.

Ethan answered, "The chocolate demonstration." Having already eaten two blueberry muffins for breakfast, he thought about how good chocolate would taste for dessert. "Do you have any more of those chocolates?" he asked Amanda.

"I'm sorry, I didn't bring any this time," she answered. Then she continued, "The point is that we need to be very specific about who we are going to target."

The elf executives nodded in agreement, but Santa was stone-faced. Though he agreed that they should be targeting kids, he was still unhappy about walking away from targeting adults. Amanda, sensitive to Santa's fears about what this work would mean for his company, sensed his reluctance to cut the production of his tie and perfume lines. "Santa," said Amanda. "Are you okay with all of this?"

Santa looked at her somberly. "No, Amanda. I think you are right. I don't think we are going to be successful at making everyone happy. We need to focus the business." The joy seemed to have escaped from Santa.

Amanda looked to the rest of the executives to help her

lift Santa's spirits. Ethan played with the muffin crumbs on his plate. In all the years they had worked together, Georgia and Simon had never seen Santa deflated, and they didn't know what to say to their boss. Finally, Melinda spoke up, "I think it's the best thing, Santa. We are going to be so loved by kids, that it will be impossible not to be loved by their parents."

"That's a great point," Amanda said. "When you target a market segment, it doesn't mean that you are excluding others as customers. It means that you are spending your time, energy, and resources on attracting your target consumers. But you will also attract others to your business as well. This phenomenon is called the Halo Effect. You get kids to love you, the parents will follow."

Santa perked up again. "So, how do we get them to believe in us again?"

"We will get them to believe in us again," Amanda assured Santa. "But first, let's figure out who our core consumer is. What I'd like us to do now is develop a description of the consumer. It doesn't reflect every consumer exactly, but in broad strokes, it is a description of the type of consumer we are targeting. Tell me, who is our consumer?"

"Well, as we discussed, they are kids between the ages of four and eight," said Georgia.

"Good," said Amanda. "What else? What do they like to do? What are their attitudes? What makes them different from other kids?"

"They are optimistic," said Ethan. "And they live in their imagination."

"That's great," said Amanda. "What you are describing

Ethan is the consumer's psychographic profile," said Amanda. She went on to explain the difference between demographics and psychographics. "Demographics refer to a consumer's basic statistics, like his age, income, gender, and measures like household makeup and occupational status. While it's important to know this information, so we know how to reach the consumer, it's just as important to understand his psychographic profile—such as a consumer's beliefs, life-style, and attitudes and behaviors about the category and the brand. Knowing a consumer's psychographic profile provides companies with better direction on how to design and market brands and products that appeal to that consumer."

"I like this idea that we get to know them as people..." said Simon, starting to warm up to the value of consumer research, though still suspicious of this whole branding process. "I'll add something. They love to play. They like to play make-believe. They like to play outside. They even play by themselves for hours."

"That's wonderful. I am starting to get an excellent picture of who these kids are," said Amanda. "What else?"

"They have dreams," added Georgia. "Just like Claudette. She wants to be an astronaut."

"Great! How do they feel about Santa?" Amanda asked.

Santa bellowed, "They love Santa!"

"They certainly do!" echoed the rest of the executives.

"They get excited when they get gifts from Santa's Workshop, and they want to one day visit here and see all the elves and reindeer for themselves. They believe in me!" Santa exclaimed.

"Right on! That's all true," Amanda said.

Amanda's face turned stern. "Okay. Now, I have to mention something else that might be a little contentious. There was a little girl who we interviewed by the name of Zelda. She was rambunctious and didn't listen to her mother. She yelled at us and even cursed at us when we were in her home. Do you remember that, Melinda?"

"Oh, my gosh, that kid was a complete terror. She almost hit me over the head with the gift that you sent to her last year, Santa. If her mother hadn't stopped her, she would have clocked me over the head with a wooden dollhouse!" Melinda exclaimed. "I'm sorry, but this is not the kind of kid who should be in our target."

"Gosh, that must have been awful," said Georgia to Melinda.

"Kids like that shouldn't be allowed on playgrounds," Ethan added. "I remember when I was a kid, some bully bit me right on the…"

"Kids are kids," interrupted Santa. "It doesn't matter if they are a little bad."

"I don't know, Santa," Georgia said. "If we are focusing our business, shouldn't we target good kids in the hopes that bad kids might see what good kids are getting? Maybe they'll want to be good too. That's what Amanda said, isn't it? She said that if we target one group, it will halo to another."

"That's exactly right," said Amanda. "Santa, I have to agree with your executives. We should target nice kids and perhaps the naughty kids will follow. After all, the elves spend countless hours making these beautiful gifts. Shouldn't they go to the most deserving kids?"

Santa squirmed in his seat. He was beginning to

understand target marketing, but it still made him uncomfortable that he would explicitly deny gifts to kids who misbehaved. While he wanted everyone to have joy, perhaps focusing on good kids would help him better fulfill his mission. Santa nodded his head slowly and agreed, "I guess my gifts should go to the most deserving."

"Well, let's take a five-minute break while I gather our notes," Amanda instructed the team.

CHAPTER 33
THE TARGET DESCRIPTION

While Amanda wrote on the Magic Pad, the rest of the group helped themselves to some more coffee, muffins, and scones. Ethan asked Santa what Mrs. Claus was making for dinner, and when Santa said it was beef stew, they all licked their lips in anticipation. The smells from the kitchen down the hall had already enveloped the boardroom with the subtle smell of herbs.

Amanda stepped away from the Magic Pad and told the group that she had summarized the team's thinking about the consumer. She created two consumers who fit the profile to bring these consumers to life. The intention was not to target market to two consumers, she added, hoping that they would not misinterpret this exercise. It was to paint a picture of the type of consumer the Workshop would target. She created an evocative title for these consumers—one that would telegraph the essence of their consumer. And she chose a picture of two kids playing in the snow, a photo she found in a magazine that she had on hand for an exercise they were going to do later in the session.

OUR CONSUMER: WISHFUL OPTIMISTS

Jasper, age 4, and his sister Andi, age 6, are fun-loving and happy kids. They are imaginative. They love toys and they like to play make-believe. Jasper and Andi love being outdoors, but they can create countless activities for themselves when they have to stay in on a rainy day.

They are good kids—always very considerate to other kids and polite to adults. They are optimistic and believe that one day they'll reach their dreams. Andi wants to be the next Amelia Earhart, and Jasper wants to be an artist.

They love getting gifts from Santa. It makes them feel special. They get excited when they talk about Santa and the little elves that help him. They want to visit the North Pole one day and ride the reindeer.

The executives listened and read the board as Amanda spoke. After Amanda finished her reading, the group fell silent. "What do you think? Do you think we've painted a good portrait of your consumer?"

No one wanted to speak first, but finally, Simon spoke up. "I can see these kids. I think it's terrific."

"Me too," said Ethan. "I like the details in the description—like the fact that Andi wants to be like Amelia Earhart. You know I wanted to work in a toy shop when I was a kid. And look at me now!"

"Yeah...I agree," said Georgia, "I really like it."

Melinda nodded with agreement, "It totally sounds like the kids we met in the research. We did a good job."

The team looked over at Santa and waited in anticipation of his reaction. He read through the words on the Magic Pad one more time, and let the words sink in. "Well," he said. The others braced themselves for his words. "I think we did a mighty fine job."

Everyone sighed with relief. There was a knock at the door, and then Mrs. Claus peered into the conference room. "Everyone ready for lunch?"

"Come in, come in," chanted the team members.

"Let's take a break, and after lunch, we'll talk about what a consumer insight is," Amanda said.

CHAPTER 34
A CONSUMER INSIGHT

After enjoying Mrs. Claus' delicious lunch of gourmet grilled gruyere sandwiches and tomato basil soup, the team was ready to get back to work. Amanda placed the Magic Paper that contained the description of the consumer "The Wishful Optimists" on the boardroom wall so that everyone could see it.

"Okay. Now that we've talked about the consumer, let's talk about what an insight is." Amanda said as she wrote words on another large piece of paper. It said:

WHAT'S A CONSUMER INSIGHT?
A deep and penetrating truth about the consumer that profoundly resonates with her

After reading the statement to the executives, Amanda asked if there were any questions about what an insight was.

"So, an insight is something that a consumer deeply connects with," Melinda restated.

"Yes. That is correct. In branding, we start with a consumer insight, and we find a way to deliver on that insight."

"Can you give us an example of an insight?" asked Georgia.

"Okay. Let's see," said Amanda. "We're all going to have Mrs. Claus' beef stew for dinner tonight. I'm presuming you've all had it before?" Amanda received exuberant head nods in return. "What would be a consumer insight about beef stew?" she asked.

"The stew is delicious!" answered Ethan excitedly.

"Well, that certainly is true. But I want to make a distinction between an observation and an insight. An observation is something you see or observe. An insight goes deeper into a desire of the consumer. It's the 'whys' beneath the observation," explained Amanda. "Why don't we try again?"

Ethan thought about Amanda's challenge but could not help but think about how delicious Mrs. Claus' stew was.

"Is an insight something like, when the weather is cold, Mrs. Claus' stew is warm and comforting?" Georgia offered.

"A consumer insight is typically stated more broadly while a positioning statement, or more specifically, what I call a brand promise, would address how a brand or product delivers on the insight. Your statement is closer to a positioning statement. With your example, an insight might be, 'When the weather is frigid, a stew is warm and comforting.' Does that make sense?"

Melinda asked, "So a consumer insight is a broad statement about the beliefs or attitudes of the consumer, and the positioning is how a brand or product addresses an insight?"

"Correct! A positioning statement that addresses Georgia's insight could be, 'Mrs. Claus' beef stew warms and comforts me—body and soul,'" Amanda explained. "We'll get to positioning a little later. Right now, I want to focus on the consumer insight. Typically, I like to write a consumer insight as a consumer quote—something that a consumer would say," said Amanda.

"What about something like, 'When times are uncertain, there is nothing more soothing than homemade comfort food,'" said Simon.

The executive team looked at Simon with curiosity. For someone very analytical, Simon was surprisingly intuitive. Simon's thoughtfulness impressed Amanda. "That is great," she said.

Santa blurted out, "Stews bring me back to my childhood."

"Excellent!" Amanda applauded Santa. "This is a crucial point. There are many consumer insights and many different ways to deliver on that insight. It's our job as brand stewards to figure out which is the most compelling insight and how we can best address the insight. Any others?"

"There is nothing more satiating and filling than a bowl of warm stew," said Melinda.

"Amen," said Ethan. Finally, understanding what a consumer insight was, he added, "I can eat stew all day because it is so good for me."

"Wonderful!" raved Amanda. "I think you all understand what a consumer insight is."

CHAPTER 35

INSIGHTS INTO THE
WISHFUL OPTIMISTS

"**L**et's think about our consumer, the Wishful Optimists. What are some interesting insights about our consumers?"

There was a very long silence. While comfortable with talking about how much they loved stew, the executives had difficulty stating insights about their target consumers.

"Come on," Amanda implored. "We just spent three weeks on the road hearing from these amazing kids, and you know everything that we've learned. What do they want? What do they desire? What are their wishes?"

There was a long silence before Melinda spoke. "Would a consumer insight be, 'I feel special and excited when I get a gift'?"

"Okay, that's great. That is an interesting insight." Amanda wrote down the insight on the Magic Pad.

"How about, 'I love the anticipation of getting and opening a gift.' The kids said they loved opening Santa's gifts," Georgia said.

"Good," Amanda said as she wrote down Georgia's comment on the Magic Pad underneath Melinda's insight. "What are other consumer insights?"

"Santa Claus brings me gifts because he wants me to be

happy and joyful," bellowed Santa.

Amanda paused before writing down Santa's words. "Okay, I want to remind everyone that an insight is broad. We will answer the insight with the brand's positioning. Let me tweak this one to fit our definition of an insight." Amanda writes, "Getting a gift makes me feel happy because I know someone cares."

Santa read the sentence to himself. "It's true. That's why I do it. It's because I care. I hope that's how kids feel."

"They do feel that way. They know you care," Amanda assured Santa. "Any others?"

"What about something around play?" asked Ethan. "Kids love to play…just like elves. How about, 'Playtime is a time for fun, discovery, and surprise.'"

"Excellent!" Amanda appreciated that the executives listened to her consumer research debrief.

"What I found interesting in the research is that kids have dreams and a belief that they will achieve them, and their parents are not always supportive," said Simon. Simon remembered his dream of helping Santa build his company. Simon's parents had disapproved of his desire to follow this peculiar, jolly, red-suited man to the North Pole to help bring joy to the world. Even his practicality could not get in the way of Santa's infectious vision.

Amanda wrote something on the board that tried to encapsulate Simon's thought: "Although parents might not agree, I still believe that anything is possible."

"How about that…does that capture it?" asked Amanda.

"Yes, that's true…anything is possible. Trucks can fly. Elves exist. We can reinvent the Workshop!" Simon bellowed, getting a bit carried away. Composing himself, he had to remind himself that he was the finance guy, the one who had to account for every dollar and cent in their operation.

Simon's consumer insight brought up an interesting point. Most of the insights they wrote down referred to children's attitudes about the category—gifts in this case. Amanda explained that a consumer insight could also be a general insight about the consumer—a deep belief that she holds. She asked the executives if they heard any other insights.

"I remembered that kids loved getting gifts that they wished for," said Melinda, recalling six-year old Sonya from New Jersey who wanted a doll with red hair just like hers. "When Sonya got that doll from Santa two years ago, she was ecstatic."

"So maybe something like, 'I believe that wishes do come true,'" Amanda said, paraphrasing Melinda. "Any others?"

They all sat back looking at the list of consumers insights that they generated for their consumers: The Wishful Optimists. "Now, which one of these insights illuminates a deep and penetrating truth?" Amanda asked.

They thought for a moment, and Santa said, "They all do. But, I like the one about the kids feeling that someone cares for them. That's the way we've always approached our relationship with kids."

"I like that one as well. But if I have to be honest, the last two we wrote are the ones that get me excited," said Georgia. "We know that believing in Santa is part of a kid's imagination and that getting a gift they wish for is exciting."

"Can we combine the last two?" asked Melinda. "To something like 'Although adults might not agree, I believe that anything is possible, and wishes do come true.'" Melinda thought about it more. "I don't think we should portray adults so negatively. Some adults want to believe that things are possible. There weren't many, but they still existed. I think we should eliminate the first phrase."

Amanda looked at the two statements and thought about it. "Normally, I would say that we should be careful about diluting a consumer insight with too many thoughts, but in this case, I think the two statements go hand in hand. And I agree with you. The beginning part about adults may be too harsh." Amanda re-wrote the last two sentences based on the team's suggestion and then stepped back.

"Any other thoughts about these insights?" asked Amanda.

"I love the last one we wrote. It sets these kids apart from other kids," said Georgia.

"I like Santa's favorite. We care about kids," said Ethan.

"I have to agree with Georgia. The last one we wrote is interesting," said Melinda. "But, I also like the one about play."

"I like the one about play too," said Georgia, "But to be honest...I don't know if we can deliver on that uniquely. We have two major competitors—JoJo's and Geppetto's, and both focus on discovery and fun."

Amanda responded to Georgia's challenge, "You have a good point. I think playtime is a major component for these kids, but perhaps its better served as a way to describe our target rather than an insight upon which to build the brand. You are right to think about which insights we can deliver on uniquely."

"Simon, what about you?" Amanda asked.

Simon tapped his pen on his pad, reluctant to answer Amanda's questions directly. "I like thinking about consumer insights. I do. But I'm still grappling with why we are going through this whole process. Can't we just say we are going to target kids? I can work with that. I know what to do. We cut our adult and teen lines, and then we…"

Amanda cut Simon short. "Simon, I'm going to ask you to trust me on this. I want you to suspend any judgment about this process until we complete the process. Can you do that for me?"

Simon nodded slowly.

On the Magic Pad, Amanda circled two of the insights that the executive team liked best:

"Getting a gift makes me feel happy because I know someone cares."

"I believe that anything is possible, and wishes do come true."

Amanda stepped back from the Magic Pad and smiled. She liked the way the group articulated the consumer insights. She turned back to the group and informed them that their next step was to build a brand blueprint. They took a short coffee break with Mrs. Claus' butter cookies and then began developing the brand.

CHAPTER 36
THE BRAND BLUEPRINT

The brand blueprint, Amanda explained, is a brand's positioning and a model to help guide marketing and communications. It provides a snapshot of the brand's strengths and its unique selling proposition or its brand promise. Just as architects use blueprints, brand builders can use this model to help instruct them on how to build their brand.

Amanda shared with the executives the components of the brand blueprint, which looked just like a house. One look at the brand blueprint and a marketer would know how to talk about the brand, and a product developer would know how to create new products to meet the needs of the consumer.

"The brand blueprint contains six critical components," explained Amanda. "First, at the foundation of the house is the consumer insight. The insight is at the foundation because it's the building block of the brand. A brand should be designed specifically to meet the needs of the consumer. In the left room of the house are the stated benefits of the brands—the specific functional and emotional benefits that compel a consumer to engage with the brand. The right side contains the reasons to believe—the support for the benefits or the substantiation for the positioning. On the very top of the house is the chimney, where we articulate the brand's personality or voice. The roof of the house is where the brand comes to together into a brand promise—the single most compelling and competitive reason for the consumer to choose the brand. And finally, at the doorway is something called the brand essence. The essence is short-hand for the brand—a few words to encapsulate what the brand means."

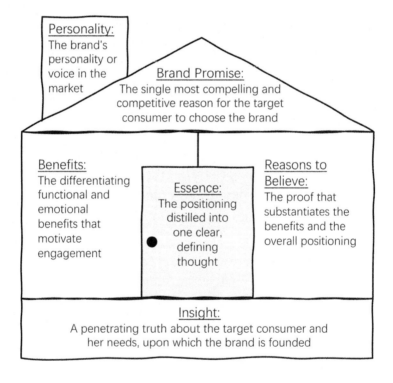

The executives had many questions about the brand blueprint, but Amanda asked them to hold their questions because next, they would talk in more depth about each element of the brand blueprint. They all agreed.

"But why is it called a brand blueprint?" asked Georgia.

"You can think of the brand blueprint as a model for the brand you want to build," she said. "Every brand should have a distinct point of view, just like your own home."

Amanda went on to describe her brownstone apartment in New York. As an avid traveler, she had collected many artifacts from around the world, including African masks, Asian rugs, and Indian carvings. Her home showcased these items in a warm and inviting atmosphere. The house contained walls painted in terracotta, amber, and burnt sienna. When she's there, she often has world music playing on the stereo. She explained how different her place was to Melinda's apartment, which she learned during their many conversations on the road featured a Country French style with antique white furniture and rococo-style paintings.

"Just as you can design a home that reflects your style, you can design a brand to reflect a specific point of view. A brand should be designed like a well-appointed home, and the plan for this home is the brand blueprint."

The executives understood now why Amanda used the metaphor of a blueprint to outline the components of the brand. It felt exciting to actually "design" a brand. Considering they didn't know the difference between a product and a brand just a short time ago, this would be quite an undertaking.

Remembering her question from their first meeting, Melinda asked again, "Amanda, is the brand Santa Claus or Santa's Workshop?"

"That's a great question. Santa's Workshop had strong associations like quality and craftsmanship. But consumers have a stronger emotional connection with Santa Claus. In my opinion, the brand should be Santa Claus."

"Does this mean we have to change our product labeling to Santa Claus?" asked Simon in a panic. "I just ordered 10,000 Santa's Workshop labels for our next production run."

"No, I don't think you need to change the way you label the products. As I said, Santa's Workshop still has great meaning for the brand, and it can still act as an endorser to the brand."

Simon and Georgia shared a collective sigh as they thought about how costly the disposal of those labels would have been. The company was already experiencing severe cash flow issues, and another unforeseen expense like new labels would have grave consequences.

Amanda could sense that the team was still a little unsure about the brand blueprint, but she also knew that once they completed it, it would make sense to them. She asked them to trust her and let her guide them through the process before they made any judgments.

The elf executives, except for Simon, who still didn't see the value of the branding process, gave their full trust to Amanda and encouraged her to proceed.

Even Santa, who was still very anxious, decided to keep an open mind and gave Amanda his approval to continue. "Let's build a new brand blueprint," he said. "Where do we start? We have two consumer insights that we liked."

"First, let's build one brand blueprint based on one of the

insights," said Amanda. "Then we can go back and build another based on the second one. Which one do you want to start with?"

When the group fell quiet, Amanda turned to the boss, "Santa, what would you like to start with?"

"Let's start with the one that others liked better—the second one," Santa said.

"Great," Amanda said, "We'll start with building a brand around the consumer insight: I believe that anything is possible, and wishes do come true. This insight will be at the foundation of our brand blueprint." She looked around the room to see the executives nodding their heads.

"Are you ready to build the Santa Claus brand blueprint?" Amanda asked.

The group tentatively sang, "Yes."

"You can do better than that," she said, giving her cheerleader best.

"Yes!" they shouted.

"Well, let's do it," she exclaimed.

CHAPTER 37
BENEFITS

Amanda pulled out a fresh sheet of paper from the Magic Pad and drew out an outline of the brand blueprint, leaving space for each of the six elements. In the base of the home, she wrote the words "Consumer Insight" and underlined it. Then below it, she wrote in quotes: "I believe that anything is possible, and wishes do come true." Then Amanda wrote in the titles of each area on the brand blueprint: benefits, reasons to believe, personality, brand promise, brand essence.

She pointed to the left side of the home and said, "Okay, think about those attributes that make your brand stand out from other brands. What benefits does the brand offer that will fulfill this consumer insight?"

The room was silent. Amanda realized this would be harder than she thought. Then she had an idea. "I'll be right back," said Amanda. She left the room, and minutes later, she was back.

"Grab your Magic Notepads and Magic Markers and follow me," instructed Amanda as she picked up an easel with Magic Paper and carried it out the door. Puzzled, the elves looked at each other, but then gathered their belongings and followed Amanda out the door.

Amanda led them down the hall into the Claus' kitchen, where Mrs. Claus was laboring over her famous stew. The executives entered the kitchen while Mrs. Claus was adding vegetables to the simmering stew.

"Hi, sweetheart," said Santa as he kissed her on the cheek. The kitchen was warm, and the smell of beef stew filled the small room. Mrs. Claus' collection of decorative porcelain plates and colorful kitchenware set a cheerful and creative atmosphere in which the team could work.

"Sit down, please," said Amanda as she pointed to the table tucked in the corner of the kitchen and set down her easel. "Mrs. Claus, we will be working, so just continue with what you were doing."

"I'll be quiet as a mouse," said Mrs. Claus. She began slicing apples for her famous apple pie that would accompany dinner.

"So, let's get back to our exercise on benefits. In the example of Mrs. Claus's beef stew, what might a benefit be?" she asked, attempting to prompt them.

The executives could taste Mrs. Claus's beef stew in their minds as it cooked on the stove.

"It's a delicious, hearty soup," said Ethan, as he licked his lips, anticipating its taste.

"Great," said Amanda. "What are some other benefits?"

"It is made with high-quality ingredients," said Georgia.

"That's wonderful. What else? These are great functional benefits of the brand. But what are some emotional benefits?"

The executives looked at Amanda blankly. "What do you mean by emotional benefits?" asked Melinda.

Amanda explained that a functional benefit usually referred to a physical attribute of the product. For example, a product could be durable, long-lasting, soft, flexible, delicious, chunky. An emotional benefit is a benefit that a consumer would feel from the experience of the product. A lock for a door could be strong and indestructible on a functional level. On an emotional level, it would also provide peace of mind and a feeling of safety and protection.

"Ah," said Santa. "Then, I would say it is comforting because it's warm."

"And it makes you feel satiated—not just physically, but emotionally too," said Ethan, licking his lips.

Amanda was pleased that the team was quickly picking up the marketing lingo. "Now, what are the benefits of the Santa Claus brand?"

The executives thought for a moment. These concepts were still new to them, and they were afraid to speak up.

Simon then stated the obvious, "We make handmade toys exclusively for kids."

"Do we have to say exclusively for kids?" asked Santa.

"We all agreed that we were going to target the Wishful Optimists," Amanda said. Amanda worried that if Santa didn't focus, he would begin to waver about his decision to limit production to kids.

"Yes, I realize that," he said tentatively, "But, can't we…"

"Santa, we have to focus if we are going to save the Workshop," Melinda interrupted. "I don't want to lose any of our sponsors." It was the first time that Melinda had been this curt with Santa. The prospect of losing her valued sponsors was stressful.

Santa sat back in his seat with a pout and said quietly, "You're right. We need to save the Workshop." He looked at

Mrs. Claus, who was rolling out dough on a large wooden cutting board at the kitchen counter and let out a sigh.

Amanda looked at the benefit and asked, "We want to make sure that the benefits and the insight are aligned. Is there anything that this sentence is missing?"

They all reread the insight. Ethan chimed in, "What about that we make handmade toys to fulfill kids' wishes."

"That's very good," Amanda replied as she revised the sentence. Ethan smiled with pride. Santa held back a grin; he didn't like to be "exclusive" and was happy to see the word disappear from the sentence. "What's another benefit?" Amanda asked.

Georgia said, "Would a benefit be something like, individual gifts that come in the mail by surprise?"

"That's great, but let's make this a little more differentiating and say that they are unique gifts that are delivered by surprise," said Amanda as she wrote down her revised words. "I like the word surprise because it adds a feeling of possibility. Is there anything else we are missing? What about emotional benefits?"

"What about the fact that we make kids happy. Isn't that the focus of the Workshop?" said Ethan. Everyone else nodded in agreement. It was so obvious, but no one had mentioned it yet.

Amanda wrote, "Make kids happy by giving them what they wish for."

"Yes, we do that, don't we?" Santa said to himself. The smile that had disappeared from his face reemerged.

CHAPTER 38
REASONS TO BELIEVE

Amanda moved on to the right side of the brand blueprint and reviewed the definition of reasons to believe. "Remember I explained that reasons to believe are the support or proof that these benefits, and overall positioning, are true," she said. "But before we talk about the Santa Claus brand, let's go back to the example of Mrs. Claus' stew. What is the supporting evidence that the benefits you mentioned are true? So, for example, what would make you believe that it's a delicious, hearty stew?"

"Mrs. Claus' secret recipe was passed down from her grandmother," Santa said. "She won't even tell me what's in the stew."

"That's right, dear," said Mrs. Claus from across the kitchen, "I will take it to my grave." She let out a chuckle, then put her index finger to her mouth, signaling that she was done speaking.

"That's wonderful," said Amanda. "A secret recipe is a good reason for people to believe that the soup is delicious and hearty. So, you also mentioned that the stew is made with high-quality ingredients. What is the proof that they are high quality?"

"Oh, I know," said Georgia. "When we first arrived at

the North Pole, Mrs. Claus' soup provided so much comfort to all the hungry, hardworking elves who built North Pole Village. The ingredients are all grown in British Columbia. That's where we had all the wood shipped from when we built the town. Mrs. Claus would ask for the freshest potatoes, turnips, and onions from the farms near the lumber yards. "

"That's an excellent support point for why the soup contains high-quality ingredients. Now, we also mentioned that it is comforting. How do you know this is true?" Amanda asked.

"Mrs. Claus makes it with tender loving care," said Ethan. "That comforts me." Everybody knew that Mrs. Claus spent hours cooking the stew because she loved the elves so much.

Mrs. Claus let out a sigh as she finished laying the latticework on two apple pies, smiling as she half-listened to the executives working.

"Okay, that's great. Now, let's talk about the Santa Claus brand." Amanda referred back to the brand blueprint.

She reviewed the benefits and asked the executives for support for each of them. "First, what supports the fact that 'Santa Claus makes handmade toys to fulfill kids' wishes?'"

"We have a state-of-the-art workshop run by our elves in the North Pole," Ethan answered. "It's super-efficient, and we have strict quality control measures...overseen by me, of course," he said with a wink.

Amanda smiled at Ethan, delighted that he understood what a reason to believe was. She wrote down his answer on the Magic Pad.

"Very good," said Amanda, "So what makes it true that

the Workshop sends surprises in the mail?"

"Oh, that's easy," said Simon. "We have a good relationship with the Canadian postal service; they make sure it gets there on time."

Amanda paraphrased Simon's explanation. She wrote, "Delivered reliably by the postal service in the mail."

"What about the fact that we make kids happy by giving them what they wish for?" said Amanda. "How do you support this idea?"

"I can answer that one," said Melinda. "We have so many things to ensure this. We have a call center and mailroom that receives letters from kids around the world. Santa keeps a list of what gifts the kids want, and we check it off every time we mail them a gift."

"Well, we only get calls from kids," said Ethan. "Adults don't call or write really. But now we don't have to worry about that."

"But we haven't been entirely good at keeping to that list—even with the kids. Remember Bobby and the underwear?" said Georgia. The group nodded in sadness, and a tear welled up in Santa's eye.

On the large Magic Paper, Amanda condensed Melinda's words into a simple statement: 'Santa's list of kids' wishes.' "So, we have to be more vigilant about keeping to this list. Furthermore, since we are only focusing on kids, we'll have an easier time keeping track. This reason to believe has got to be non-negotiable for the brand. That's why we write it down in the brand blueprint."

Amanda stood back and looked at the list of benefits and reasons to believe that they had developed and then nodded her head. Amanda was glad that they had taken a trip to the kitchen to mix things up. Using Mrs. Claus' stew to help them think of benefits and reasons to believe was a useful exercise.

"Good job, everyone. Let's go back into the boardroom. We can take a break before we get to the next order of business—the brand's personality."

The executives were sent back to the boardroom with a plate of chocolate chip cookies and milk. The executives gathered around the boardroom window with their cookies to take in the picture-perfect day and the white snow that glistened in the sun. The clock tower in the middle of town chimed three times, and the doors of the workshop flung open. The elves on the first shift began listlessly emptying into the village square. They stretched and yawned, and then headed their separate ways, as a new group of elves began entering the grand wooden doors into the workshop.

The executives watched the shift change with heartbreak. There was a time when the elves would run into the village square and leap for joy for having fulfilled another kid's wish with a beautiful handmade gift. Santa gave out a sigh of sadness and then sat back down in his seat, anxious to continue working on the brand blueprint.

CHAPTER 39
AN ALI BABA BREAK

T he executives came back to their seats, looking sluggish and tired as if they had just worked a shift along with the elves in the workshop. Amanda had to do something to lift their spirits and give them energy.

Amanda did as she always did during brand sessions like this one—she got everyone to stand in a circle and do a few rounds of the *Ali Baba and the Forty Thieves* game. Ethan stood to her right, followed by Melinda, Georgia, and Simon. Santa stood to Amanda's left to complete the circle.

To make the game more personal, she asked Ethan how many people worked at the company. He answered, "Sixty-one." Then Amanda gave them the instructions for the game. She would make a gesture, like pat her head with her hand, while simultaneously singing the words, "Santa Claus and the sixty-one elves" to the tune of *Ali Baba and the Forty Thieves*. Then, once she finished the gesture, the person to her right, Ethan, needed to copy her exactly. Simultaneously, Amanda would then work on a second gesture. Once Ethan finished with the first gesture, the person to his right, Melinda, had to make the first gesture while Ethan imitated Amanda's second gesture. And so on.

Amanda began the game with her first move. She pulled

on her imaginary suspenders, in honor of Santa, while chanting, "Santa Claus and the sixty-one elves" together with the executives. For her next move, she shrugged her shoulders up and kicked her feet up. She made several other moves, all while watching the executives try to follow the person to their left and simultaneously chant, "Santa Claus and the sixty-one elves." The look of determination filled the faces of the elves and Santa. The group appeared to be getting the hang of it except for Simon, who was the most uncoordinated of the bunch. He made many mistakes, and as a result, Santa, the last person in the circle, messed up royally too.

When the players took notice of Santa's flailing gestures, they began to giggle. The giggles turned into laughter, and the laughter turned into howling. A group of elves gathered to watch the spectacle from outside the window of Santa's boardroom. Simon, who was usually very reserved, was on his back, holding his stomach and rolling around on the floor, giddy with laughter. Even Melinda, who was typically very poised, let down her inhibitions and began snorting, which made everyone laugh even harder. Amanda, who was trying to keep herself composed and professional in front of her clients, keeled over and cried with delight. Santa's ho-ho-ho turned into hee-hee-hee as he gasped for breath in between words.

After letting it all out, the group slowly composed themselves. They slumped back into the leather chairs around the old oak table, with smiles of content on their faces.

"Well, it's been ages since we've heard laughter like that in this room," said Santa. "Thank you, Amanda," he added.

Amanda smiled, hoping that she was finally breaking through to Santa. She remembered her first meeting with him. This Santa was very different. Perhaps he was starting to feel a little more joy since the start of his business problems, Amanda wondered to herself. She hoped that happiness was beginning to come back to Santa's Workshop and that it would stay for good this time.

CHAPTER 40
THE BRAND'S PERSONALITY

There was still a lot of work to be done. Amanda tried to get everyone to focus after the much-needed distraction of the *Santa Claus and the Sixty-one Elves* game. "That game surely brought out everyone's personality. Now, let's get to the next order at hand. Let's define the personality of the brand. I know this may sound odd to you at first, but how can a brand have a personality?"

That's precisely what everyone in the room was thinking.

"Remember, we are not trying to create a product. What did we say about products? Products are a lot like commodities. They are easily substituted. What we are trying to do here is to create a brand. All brands have personalities, and they elicit an emotional response from the consumer."

"It's strange to think that brands have personalities," said Simon. Simon's politeness in delivering his statement struck Amanda. At the beginning of the session, he would have dismissed the idea of brands having personalities, but perhaps he is now warming up to the concept of branding.

"All great, memorable brands have a personality. If you think about every brand that you come into contact with, you can describe it just like you describe a person. You don't even have to see advertising to determine a brand's personality.

You can get a sense of a brand's personality by the product experience or even by its packaging alone," explained Amanda. The team looked baffled, having never considered that the Santa Claus brand could have a personality.

Amanda asked, "Let's talk about those Fifer hats that we talked about earlier. What are some words to describe the brand's personality?"

"Rugged," Ethan said, pulling his hat off his head and feeling the sturdy material.

"Also, approachable," Georgia added.

"Strong," said Santa, as he looked at the hat on Simon's head.

"Whimsical," said Melinda, impressing herself with her choice of words.

"Whimsical?" said Ethan. "Why do you say that?"

"Because," she explained, "each hat features a different feather on it—presumably from different types of birds. See Georgia's hat has a feather that's purple and yellow with a big aqua blue circle on the top. I think hers must be a peacock feather. Ethan, yours is black with white around the edges and a big red stripe in the middle. And Simon's is dark green, fades to olive green and then turns bright blue on the tip and has spots of yellow all over it. That's fun. It's whimsical."

Amanda nodded her head in agreement, "That is fantastic, Melinda. I love your choice of words. The more evocative the words we pick, the better our brand blueprint. I think we all have the hang of it. What words would you use to describe the Santa Claus brand? Let's come up with our list and pick the best words to describe the brand's personality."

The executives nodded in agreement while Amanda

prepared a fresh piece of Magic Paper and picked up a Magic Marker. When the group began throwing words out to Amanda, she wrote as fast as she could.

PERSONALITY

- Friendly
- Fun
- Playful
- Delightful
- Humorous
- Happy
- Merry
- Warm
- Homemade
- Caring
- Silly
- Creative
- Funny
- Joyful
- Quality
- Collaborative
- Congenial
- Expressive
- Comforting

After a while, the group started to repeat themselves, and Amanda knew it was time to stop brainstorming. She stepped back and reflected on the list.

"I think we are missing a word." She returned to the list and wrote at the bottom, "Magical."

The group nodded in agreement.

"This is the first thing I thought to myself when I came here. When I met the elves and rode those incredible reindeer, I thought to myself that this is a magical place."

Then Amanda asked the group to pick out the most evocative words. She also asked them to consider which words were similar and which words were better than the others. For example, they talked about silly, funny, happy, joyful, and merry. They all described a type of personality. But when they thought about it, they thought silly was too over-the-top. Funny didn't quite represent the brand. Between happy, joyful, and merry, they liked merry and joyful best because it was more exuberant that happy. Homemade, comforting, and warm were also very similar, and the team decided that warm resonated the most with them.

They continued to discuss the words, and in the end, they decided on the list:

PERSONALITY
Delightful
Magical
Joyful
Playful
Warm

They liked the words on the list because they evoked a feeling.

"Ha," Ethan observed, "Those words can be used to describe Santa."

"That's very interesting," Amanda said. "It doesn't surprise me that a brand would have the same characteristics as the entrepreneur who created the brand. But this doesn't necessarily have to be the case. Those Fifer hats, for example, I believe, were created by a group of Swedish Nuns."

Amanda looked at the clock. It was approaching four o'clock, and they still had several more things to do before they called it a day. Coming up were two of the most important parts of the brand blueprint: the brand promise and the brand essence.

CHAPTER 41
BRAND PROMISE

The next part of the brand blueprint that Amanda wanted the executives to focus on was the brand promise. "A brand promise is a promise that the brand makes to consumers that fulfills their needs. It's how the brand will uniquely fit into their lives and address the insight."

She reminded the executives of the consumer insight they were trying to address: "I believe that anything is possible, and wishes do come true.'"

"Now, in thinking about the consumer insight, how does the Santa Claus brand answer a consumer's needs? How does the brand do this better than everyone else?" asked Amanda.

The group took a minute to think about Amanda's challenge. They were silent. It was hard for them to imagine picking one thing that addressed their consumer's needs better than anyone else. The team sat in silence for a long time and read the insight over and over again, "I believe that anything is possible, and wishes do come true.'"

"What I like about this insight," said Simon, breaking the silence, "Is that it talks about believing. In the research, it was so clear. Kids believed in Santa, and parents didn't.

There is something magical about our brand that no other brand can claim—not JoJo's or Geppetto's."

Surprised by his comment, Amanda thought to herself that Simon was, in fact, very creative and clever when he wasn't focusing just on the numbers. She said aloud, "That was very astute of you, Simon. I agree with you. Kids have to have faith to believe that they will get what they want. They wish for a gift and hope they get it."

"And I think that the other thing that you have to believe as a kid is that you are special," said Ethan. He smiled as he thought about how each person in the room was exceptional.

Melinda wrote on her pad as the rest of the group thought about the challenge. "What about," reading from her pad: "Believing in Santa Claus is a belief that you are special, and wishes do come true."

Amanda asked Melinda to repeat the sentence as she scribed it quickly on the Magic Paper. Then she took a step back and smiled. "Well, I think that is certainly true. Do you think this is differentiating? Can anyone claim this?"

"I don't think anyone else can claim this," said Georgia.

The others nodded their heads in agreement. The brand promise felt unique, relevant, and, most of all, differentiating. They knew that they were getting closer to a compelling articulation about what the Santa brand meant. The brand was starting to feel like a real concept, not a general idea.

CHAPTER 42
A BRAND'S ESSENCE

During the break, the executives went outside to get a breath of fresh air. They stood at the doorway of Santa's home and took in the sights and sounds of the village. The elves toiled in the workshop, an hour into the second shift. The reindeer hooves crunched in the hardened snow after a late afternoon ride in the skies, Reindeer Master Aidan's "Whoa…" adding to the chorus. The melodious sounds lulled the executives into a joyful trance.

Amanda had hung up all the paper that she had written on throughout the day. There was so much paper that she had to cover up part of the large window that overlooked the village square. Looking over the work they had created, Amanda was beginning to get excited about the prospects of the brand.

The executives came back to the old oak table and sat down. On a new sheet of Magic Paper, Amanda had drawn out the brand blueprint. It looked like this:

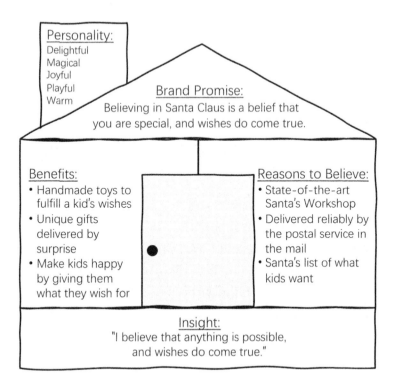

Personality:
Delightful
Magical
Joyful
Playful
Warm

Brand Promise:
Believing in Santa Claus is a belief that
you are special, and wishes do come true.

Benefits:
• Handmade toys to
  fulfill a kid's wishes
• Unique gifts
  delivered by
  surprise
• Make kids happy
  by giving them
  what they wish for

Reasons to Believe:
• State-of-the-art
  Santa's Workshop
• Delivered reliably by
  the postal service in
  the mail
• Santa's list of what
  kids want

Insight:
"I believe that anything is possible,
and wishes do come true."

Amanda presented back to the team what they had created and asked them for any feedback.

"Ho, Ho, Ho! I think it looks great!" bellowed Santa. "I
can feel the brand come alive. I feel so much more invigo-
rated now than ever before!"

The executives smiled, happy that their fearless leader
finally understood the merits of focusing.

"Now, we need to come up with a brand essence,"
Amanda announced.

"A what?" the team cried out in unison.

"A brand essence. A brand essence is a shorthand for the
brand. It's a rallying call for the brand. If you had only a few

words to describe your brand, how would you do it?"

The group looked at Amanda blankly. It had been a long day already, and the fatigue was beginning to set it. Amanda realized that she needed an example. "Wait one minute again," she said as she ran out the door. The executives looked at each other, wondering what kind of field trip they were going on now.

After a few minutes, Amanda reemerged and held the door open as Mrs. Claus wheeled in a cart with a steaming porcelain pot of beef stew on it. Mrs. Claus ceremoniously opened the lid of the pot and the room filled with the robust and delectable aroma of beef, parsnips, rosemary, and thyme. She scooped a big spoonful of beef stew loaded with potatoes, carrots, onions, and parsnips into small bowls and laid a bowl of soup in front of each person.

"Okay. Take a bite out of Mrs. Claus' beef stew and then close your eyes."

They spooned out a bit of stew and tasted it. The executives closed their eyes while Amanda spoke. "You put a spoonful of Mrs. Claus' beef stew into your mouth. It tastes so yummy and warm. You can taste all the delicious ingredients. It's chock full of vegetables grown from British Columbia. It has hearty beef in it. When you eat a bowl of this soup, you imagine yourself sitting at a farmer's table. At the table, you feel completely at home. You feel like you belong."

Ethan sniffled a little thinking about home, and the others smiled in recognition of the homey feeling. Amanda asked them, "What are a few words that capture Mrs. Claus' beef stew."

Melinda opened her eyes.

"Ah! Keep your eyes closed!" Amanda yelled out. Melinda shut her eyes quickly.

"What words come to mind?" she asked.

As they thought about the delicious stew, the words started trickling out of the executives. Amanda wrote down their descriptors.

Mrs. Claus' Beef Stew Essence:
- Succulent goodness
- Homemade warmth
- A bowl full of goodness
- Farmer's delight
- Farm in your bowl
- Fresh and fragrant
- Hearth and homemade
- At the farmer's table

When Amanda finished writing the last suggestion, she asked the group to open their eyes. "I think you have the hang of it. We have some amazing words to describe Mrs. Claus' beef stew."

"But which one is right?" said Simon, always needing to know the answer.

"Well, I don't know. Which one feels right based on the description I gave you at the beginning of this exercise?"

The group voted on the two they liked the best—'At the farmer's table' and 'Bowl full of goodness.' Amanda explained that the brand essence would depend on the positioning. 'At the farmer's table' would describe a positioning based on its wholesome, fresh from the farm ingredients, which was closer to the direction she was steering them in with her description. But 'Bowl full of goodness' was a good essence for a soup brand positioned as a healthy stew.

"Maybe we should package Mrs. Claus' soup and sell it in the market!" beamed Santa Claus. "We've already worked out the brand positioning."

"Let's just focus on one thing at a time," warned Georgia.

"Yes, of course," Santa said with a gleam in his eye. That will be in their long-term plans, he thought to himself. He knew better than to share this idea with the rest of the team.

Before they moved on to the next exercise, Amanda let the team take a break to enjoy Mrs. Claus' dinner. The executives sat around the old oak table and ate in silence as they thought about how they were going to reinvent Santa's Workshop. The velvety smooth stew warmed them as hope filled their souls.

CHAPTER 43
SANTA'S BRAND ESSENCE

"**N**ow, let's think of Santa Claus. What is the brand's essence?"

Amanda stood at the front of the room for a long time, looking at the blank faces of the executives. She knew they needed a little bit of help.

"Close your eyes," she instructed them. "You are a little kid. Your name is Joshua, and you want a reindeer stuffed animal—one that looks just like Santa's reindeer at the North Pole. You draw a picture of it in class and show it to your mother. Your mother suggests that you write a letter to Santa to ask for a toy reindeer. So, you do. 'Dear Santa, My name is Joshua, and I am a good kid. I am nice to my sister Sophie, even though she sometimes takes my things. And I always listen to my mom. Please send me a stuffed animal of my favorite animal—a reindeer. They are so cool! I hear that you have twelve real reindeer at the North Pole. That's even cooler!—Joshua.'

"Santa receives the letter and writes Joshua's request down on his list. The request then gets sent to the workshop. Elves in the stuffed animal division begin working right away on this toy, which, though Joshua doesn't know it, actually flies in the air with a remote control. Every other day for the next month, Joshua asks his mom if she thinks Santa got his letter. And every other day, his mom replies the same way, 'Santa is very busy.' But after a month, his mom replies differently to Joshua's question. She tells him that Santa has already gotten his letter, and he needs to be patient. Upon hearing this, every night before he goes to bed, Joshua says a prayer: 'I wish I get my reindeer soon.'

"Every night for two months, he says the same wish. Then one day, it comes true. In the mail comes a big box with brown wrapping paper. He rips the paper and opens the box. He throws the white tissue paper in the air, trying to find the gift. Inside is a beautiful reindeer—tan with white spots—and a remote control. Joshua jumps up and down with joy. He puts the reindeer on the ground and aims the remote control at it. When he pushes the green button on the control, the reindeer starts to ascend into the air. Joshua jumps up and down and says, 'It flies...it flies!' He thinks about Santa and how kind he is. He believes in him more than ever. Believing in Santa Claus is a belief that you are special, and wishes do come true."

The executives were mesmerized by Amanda's story, lost in the visualization of Joshua opening his present. Their flying reindeer was one of their most popular toys produced last year, thanks to the brilliant suggestion of Reindeer Master Aidan.

"What two to four words would you use to describe Santa Claus?" Amanda asked the executives.

With their eyes still closed, they started shouting out suggestions.

"Delightful surprise."

"The gift of giving."

"A box of smiles."

"The magic of giving."

"Surprise in the mail."

"Giving and receiving."

"Things that fly."

Simon opened his eyes to see who said the last statement, but Amanda reprimanded him, "Ah...close your eyes." It must have been Ethan, thought Simon.

"Acts of kindness."

"Believe in giving."

"Believe in miracles."

"That's it!" cried Santa. "That's it...the last one you said. Who said that? Oh, never mind. I like that. I like that everyone should believe in miracles. Miracles are magical. I love it!"

"But does it address the positioning? I see how it fits the 'wishes fulfilled' part. What about the 'special' aspect of the positioning?" asked Simon.

"Miracles are special and they happen because we are all special," said Santa.

"He's absolutely right," said Melinda.

"He is," agreed Georgia.

"I like the one about things flying," said Ethan.

"I knew it was you!" said Simon.

"We have a fantastic list, and I can see so many of these words fitting with the brand blueprint. For now, I'm going to put 'Believe in Miracles' in the brand blueprint, and we can continue to discuss it," said Amanda conclusively. She wrote the new brand essence into the center of the home.

Amanda looked around the room, and she saw that everyone's energy was waning. Then there was a knock at the door. "Are you ready for dessert?" asked Mrs. Claus.

"Yes!" roared the executives in unison.

Holding two apple pies in her hands, Mrs. Claus pushed the door open with her body and set them on the sideboard. The executives deserved a warm piece of pie for all their hard work, thought Amanda.

CHAPTER 44
ANOTHER BRANDING EXERCISE

Amanda looked at her watch. It was almost six p.m., and the sun was shining brightly. The Summer Solstice having passed only a few weeks before, the days were still long and bright. "I know it's been a long day… but we need to do our second brand blueprint before I let you go."

Looking around at the weary executives, she made a suggestion. "Santa, do you mind if we go into the living room to do this next exercise? I think it would be good to get a new perspective."

Santa agreed, and the entire team took their notebooks and Magic Notepads with them into the Claus' cozy living room. Sitting on the matching plaid sofa and armchairs, the executives settled into their spots around the big stone fireplace, which held a few logs of wood waiting for the next cold spell to hit the North Pole.

Amanda placed a new sheet of Magic Paper on the easel in front of the room. She then guided the executives through the other brand blueprint—this time focusing on the second consumer insight statement they had developed: "Getting a gift makes me feel happy because I know someone cares."

The development of the brand blueprint was much easier

this time around. The executives understood all the essential elements needed to develop it. They had a healthy debate over the benefits and reasons to believe. Some of them overlapped with the first brand blueprint they had developed, but some were unique to the insight that they articulated. The personality of the brand was the same, and that made sense to them.

They struggled with coming up with a compelling brand promise based on the insight, as many of the statements they developed could be said by any number of their competitors—like Geppetto's or Jack & Jill. The two things that differentiated their brand was Santa's mission to bring joy to the world through toys and the element of surprise. They developed a brand promise that said: "Santa Claus brings joy around the world with toys delivered by surprise."

They realized that their consumer insight wasn't very compelling. After some debate, they revised the statement to read: "Getting a gift I wished for brings me joy because I know someone cares." This statement then felt better because Santa Claus could deliver on this insight uniquely. They also revised the benefits and reasons to believe to include the unique aspects of Santa's gift-giving philosophy and developed a brand essence around this idea.

With all the revisions accounted for, Amanda revealed the brand blueprint:

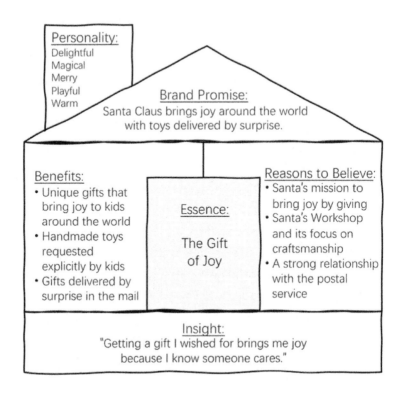

Personality:
Delightful
Magical
Merry
Playful
Warm

Brand Promise:
Santa Claus brings joy around the world
with toys delivered by surprise.

Benefits:
• Unique gifts that bring joy to kids around the world
• Handmade toys requested explicitly by kids
• Gifts delivered by surprise in the mail

Essence:

The Gift of Joy

Reasons to Believe:
• Santa's mission to bring joy by giving
• Santa's Workshop and its focus on craftsmanship
• A strong relationship with the postal service

Insight:
"Getting a gift I wished for brings me joy
because I know someone cares."

CHAPTER 45
PICKING A BRAND DIRECTION

There was one last thing that Amanda needed the executives to do before she could let them go for the evening—and that was to pick a brand direction. Amanda shuffled everyone back into the boardroom and then hung the new brand blueprint next to the one they created earlier in the day. With the two brand blueprints side by side, she asked the group to study them, as she was ready to solicit comments and reflections about them. She read the two brand promises out loud:

"Believing in Santa Claus is a belief that you are special, and wishes do come true."

"Santa Claus brings joy around the world with gifts delivered by surprise."

They let the brand promises sink in, and there was a long silence before someone spoke up.

"The first positioning we created doesn't talk about the gifts. Isn't that what we are selling, for lack of a better word?" asked Simon.

"I don't know…are you creating products, or are you creating an experience?" asked Amanda.

"What do you mean?" asked Melinda.

"Well, do you think the Santa Claus brand begins and ends with the gift? Or is it a consideration that begins with the belief that Santa Claus exists?" asked Amanda.

"It begins with the belief," answered Ethan. The rest of the executive team nodded their heads.

"It's okay to have a positioning statement that doesn't have the specific category or type of products you quote, unquote sell. The more compelling and unique a brand is, the more you can position on an emotional level." Amanda explained. She could see that the team was having a hard time understanding this concept, so she elaborated.

"Remember the Fifer hats we discussed earlier? What do you think their positioning is?" she asked.

"Something like, 'Fifer makes the most durable, long-lasting hats made especially for elves," said Georgia

"I'd include something about their uniqueness. Every hat is unique," said Melinda. "Oh, and also, they are handwoven."

"What about something like, 'Fifer's one-of-a-kind hats for elves are handwoven to last a lifetime,'" said Amanda.

Georgia smiled, "You really have a way with words, Amanda. That feels so much more descriptive."

"Thank you," said Amanda. "My point here is that we included 'hats' in the positioning because that is the category they compete it. Now, what if they decide to compete in clothing or accessories? They can still be true to their brand. If the brand were to expand to other categories, their brand promise might be: 'Fifer's one-of-a-kind wearables for elves are handmade to last a lifetime.'"

"That makes sense. I could see them making more stuff

like outerwear and boots," said Simon. "I'd bet they'd make perfect boots."

"What if they decide they need to grow and they want to get into categories even further out from hats? What if they want to get into home goods like blankets and linens? Maybe even furniture? What then?" Amanda asked the executives.

The executives looked at Amanda blankly.

"Well, I'd venture to say that they'd have to position more on an emotional level," said Amanda. "Although they can't forget about their heritage in durability, they might want to create a brand promise that focuses more on uniqueness. They already have unique hats with their whimsical feathers. So, perhaps their brand positioning could read something like, 'Fifer believes that your uniqueness shines through the quality goods you own.'" Amanda made a disclaimer that she was making up these positionings on the spot and purely for illustrative purposes. The example, she said, demonstrated that the more emotionally a company positions its brand, the more the brand can stretch.

Amanda asked the executives if they understood her explanation about brand stretch, and the executives nodded yes.

CHAPTER 46
SANTA'S BRAND PROMISE

"**N**ow. Looking back at these two brand promise statements, which one feels like it's more ownable and differentiating?" asked Amanda. She reread the statements:

"Believing in Santa Claus is a belief that you are special, and wishes do come true."

"Santa Claus brings joy around the world with gifts delivered by surprise."

Amanda looked around the room. The executives quietly sat while they waited for Santa to speak first. Picking up on the nervous glances going around the old oak table, Amanda finally asked, "Which one speaks to you, Santa?"

"I hate to say it because I was really in the joyful camp, but I like the first one because there is an element of imagination and optimism in it. It just feels better," said Santa.

Santa's comment gave license for others to speak. Georgia said, "The first one tugs at my heart. The second one also feels good, but not as much."

"I think I'm special," said Ethan. He thinks for a moment longer and shakes his head, "Yeah..., I'm special."

"I think the first one makes more sense to me because we don't just make gifts, we also sell licenses, and if I'm thinking about my part of the business, I think the first one is broader," said Melinda.

"That's an excellent point, Melinda. It's important that we make sure our positioning resonates with our corporate sponsors as well as our core target," said Amanda. Amanda explained how she felt the overall brand positioning for Santa Claus should focus on the kids because the kids will drive growth for the Workshop. And as the sponsors divulged in their interviews, they were most interested in ensuring that the kids were happy. Focusing the brand messaging on the kids would appeal to the sponsors just as much as the kids.

"This tool should be considered a master brand positioning that you base your brand design off of," she continued. "But for the corporate sponsors, the target consumer profile will be different, and how you market or activate your brand will be different as well. But the main tenets of the brand, this brand blueprint, will be consistent." Then Amanda promised Melinda that they would develop an activation strategy built off the brand blueprint that addresses the corporate clients' needs.

"How about you, Simon? What do you think?" asked Amanda, hoping that Simon had not thought the whole day was a waste.

"I'm beginning to see how helpful it is to use either of these brand blueprints to focus the business," said Simon.

Amanda was relieved, but she still didn't get her answer. She waited to see if Simon would continue, but he looked down and started tapping his pen on his notepad.

"It's late," said Amanda as she looked at her watch. She could tell the team was exhausted. She was exhausted. "What I am hearing is that we all agree that the first brand blueprint that we've developed is the most compelling direction for the brand. Is everyone comfortable with moving forward with the 'Believe in Miracles' brand area?" she asked.

All of the executives, all but Simon, had smiles on their faces and shook their heads in agreement.

"Great job, everyone! Now get a good night's sleep, and we'll pick this up in the morning," Amanda instructed the team.

The elves got up from their seats and gathered their belongings, while Santa sat in his chair deep in thought. As Amanda began organizing all the output from the session, Simon left quietly while the other elves left chattering about the new direction for the brand.

CHAPTER 47
A LEADER'S GUT

S anta watched as Amanda cleaned up the room and then approached her. "Amanda, I must say..." he began before he realized that he had startled her.

"Oh, gosh. Sorry, Santa, I didn't see you there," she said.

"I feel good about this, Amanda. I wasn't very keen on this branding thing, as you know. But I'm beginning to think that this process is valuable."

"Good, I'm glad," said Amanda as she smiled at Santa. Then she went back to cleaning up the dirty paper cups scattered on the table. Anxious to get back to the Chocolate Hotel, Amanda wanted to take a long bath and order a piece of chocolate cake from room service. The day was mentally taxing, and Amanda couldn't wait to put on her fluffy white robe and warm wool slippers.

"There is still something a little off. I'm not sure what it is, but there is still something..." Santa's words trailed off. He had difficulty trying to articulate what felt wrong.

"Do you think we're off track, Santa?" asked Amanda, now worried by Santa's concerns.

"No. I think we are on track. It feels intuitively right. That's not it," Santa said, the wrinkles on his forehead growing deeper. "I can't put my finger on it, but there's just something nagging at me."

"Well, why don't you sleep on it, and we can discuss it in the morning? It might help us to think about this when we are fresh and well-rested," Amanda suggested.

Amanda had done this exercise with many of her clients, and she knew that executives often felt a tinge of fear as they embarked on a new direction for their brand. She was confident that they would be able to alleviate Santa's concern when they discussed it tomorrow. But still, his words made her feel uneasy.

Santa nodded and then got his red jacket from the seat that he was sitting in. "I liked sitting in a new seat today, Amanda. That was a good suggestion," he said with humility.

"I'm glad, Santa. You did a great job today. Thanks for contributing. And thanks for your patience," Amanda said.

"No, it's you who did a great job. Thanks for being here." Santa turned around and hobbled out of the room, sore from sitting down all day.

Amanda watched as Santa exited the room, grinning as she thought about the possibility that the brand they'd created might come to life one day. She looked at the brand blueprint and studied the words. "Is Santa right?" she wondered. "Maybe we can do better."

She finished tidying up the room and then turned off the light. Amanda looked back into the room, scanning the large sheets of Magic Paper lining the perimeter. Lit by the low sun that streamed through the large boardroom window, the brand blueprint luminously glowed in the summer evening light. "One more day," she said, hopeful that the company might be able to rise from this crisis.

CHAPTER 48
A BRAND NEW DAY

Amanda dreamed about an imaginary town with chocolate rivers and candy-laid streets. Wherever she walked, she could reach out and eat the items. When she woke up, Amanda realized that she was in her room at the Chocolate Hotel, smelling the chocolate and banana crepes being served for breakfast downstairs. She quickly got dressed and got ready for the second and final day of the brand work session with Santa's executive team.

When she arrived at the boardroom, Amanda turned on the light and surveyed the room, making sure that everything was as she had left it. Outside, through the big window overlooking the village square, in the early morning hustle, the first of the elves entered the workshop for their morning shift. She looked at her watch; she had only a few minutes before the executives arrived.

As she thought about the agenda for the day, Amanda noticed a photo on the wall. It was the same one in Santa's office—a photo of Santa with Georgia and Simon in an empty vista of snow, standing next to a red and white pole with a wood placard that read "The North Pole." She looked out the window and saw the same pole in the middle of the square. She looked back and forth from the photo to the village square, to make sure that the pole was the same one in the picture—it was.

Remarkable, thought Amanda, noticing how a bustling and beautiful little village now filled the space. For the first time, she realized how high the stakes were in this project; Santa and his team had made an enormous emotional and financial investment in the North Pole. More than ever, she felt determined to help them turn around the company and put the spring back in the elves' steps.

Georgia arrived first in the boardroom. She ran up to Amanda and said excitedly, "I am so happy because I realized how much more focused we are going to be. I got some sleep last night. After nights of worrying about the Workshop, I finally got some sleep."

Simon and Ethan arrived next, having come from the reindeer barn where Aidan was tending to a pregnant reindeer about to give birth.

"It's so exciting. A new reindeer is coming," said Ethan.

Simon just shrugged his shoulders, "I guess so."

Melinda walked into the boardroom with Santa. They were discussing the plans to go back to the corporate sponsors and unveil their new brand identity. For the first time since Amanda had met her, Melinda wore a smile on her face.

"We have a lot of work to do," said Amanda as she called the meeting to order. Walking over to the old oak table, Santa sat in the seat that Simon sat in yesterday, an act that made Amanda smile, an act that signaled Santa was finally breaking out of his old patterns. The rest of the executives followed Santa's example and found new seats to sit in at the table.

Mrs. Claus entered with coffee and banana bread. "My favorite!" exclaimed Ethan, as he dove into the plate first.

"Mrs. Claus, your beef stew is very famous," Amanda said. "And we can't wait for lunch today!"

"Well, I have a fun surprise for you…something they say is very popular in New York. It was a special request from everyone here."

Amanda was intrigued. She missed New York, as she'd been on the road for the last month traveling across the world for research. "I can't wait," said Amanda.

Closing the door behind her, Mrs. Claus left the executives to their work, and Santa Claus exclaimed, "Now that's my lady!"

CHAPTER 49
COMPETITIVE CONTEXT

"**O**kay, let's get back to our task. Yesterday, we created a consumer portrait, and then we created a brand blueprint. Before we go any further, something occurred to me last night, and that was that we haven't yet articulated our competition."

The executives looked at Amanda skeptically. "Well, that's easy," said Melinda. "Our competitors are JoJo's Building Blocks, Geppetto's, and Jack & Jill's."

Amanda wrote the words "competitive set" on the Magic Paper and then wrote down the three toy companies.

"So, the competitive set are other toy companies?" said Amanda.

"Is this a trick question?" asked Georgia.

"No, it's not. Yes, Santa's Workshop competes with toy companies in the marketplace. But, I want you to expand your definition of your competitive set. I want you to think about the other 'competition' that you have."

"What do you mean by that?" said Simon. "These are the competitors against which we measure ourselves. We distribute more toys than any of these other companies." Simon pulled out his presentation on the market share of their toys. "See," he said, pointing to the biggest slice of pie in the chart.

"I know you think of your competition as other companies that make the same products as you, and I agree, these are your primary competitors. I also want you to consider the other moments that you compete with in a consumer's life. What would be the next best thing to opening a present from Santa?"

The executives were very quiet. They didn't understand this idea that their competition could be anything other than another toy company.

Amanda wrote the words "Competitive Context" on the Magic Pad and then underlined it. Then she listed three statements underneath it.

- Riding a two-wheeler bike for the first time
- Going to the amusement park
- Getting a visit from the tooth fairy

She stepped back for a moment and let the executives read what she wrote. She went on to explain that the words written on the Magic Pad are other magical moments in a child's life. "It's easy to think of product competitors. But the experience around the product is just as important as the product itself. So, thinking about it in this way, getting a gift from Santa is theoretically competing against different life moments."

"So, what you are saying is that we need to think not just of our product, but the experience of our product for a child," said Melinda, clarifying Amanda's explanation.

"Yes. For example, going to an amusement park is not an

everyday event. It's something special, something that's fun and surprising. It is just as joyful and exciting as getting a gift from Santa," explained Amanda.

Amanda was undoubtedly challenging the executives to think outside of their industry. They were beginning to understand this idea that getting a gift from Santa was a special moment that might be different than a JoJo's moment or a Geppetto's moment.

Santa added his own: "How about watching a reindeer fly."

Amanda smiled, knowing that Santa understood her point. She wrote it down.

Melinda, who watched the history-making voyage of Apollo 11 a week before, said, "Landing on the moon."

"Yes! The Americans walked on the moon. That was so magical!" Ethan exclaimed. The other elves nodded their heads in agreement.

Amanda wrote down the suggestions and then stepped back. "I think you get the point. I want to encourage you to not only think about your competition but also think about your competitive context."

Amanda could tell from the last exercise that the executives were wide-eyed and ready to work. She pulled the Magic Paper off of the easel pad and discovered that there was so much paper covering the walls, not a spare inch was left. Rearranging the other posters on the walls, Amanda made room for the Magic Paper.

"It's time to move on," she said as she returned to the front of the easel.

CHAPTER 50
BRAND VALUES

"**N**ow, let's get to the next order of business. I want us to talk about our values," said Amanda.

"What's a value?" asked Santa.

"It's a mathematical term. It means a quantity or a number represented by a figure or a symbol. Like the value of x," said Simon matter-of-factly. "Or it means an approximation. For example, the North Pole is valued at one million dollars."

"That's true. It is a mathematical term. But a value in sociology means the ideals or beliefs of a culture. We have to think of our brand as imbuing itself with a set of beliefs by which it abides. Values help a brand separate itself from other brands, and it also guides us, as brand stewards, on how we treat our consumers and each other."

"I'm not sure I understand," said Ethan, already on his second helping of banana bread.

"Let me see if I can come up with an example," said Amanda. She thought for a while and wondered if she should talk about Fifer hats or Mrs. Claus' stew. After a few moments, she came up with a new example. "What are the values of the City of New York? It's been on my mind lately."

Also missing the City, Melinda spoke first, "It values creativity. When I think of New York, I think of Broadway, music, and movies."

"That's good," said Amanda. "What other words come to mind when you think of New York."

"Welcoming," said Santa. "I think of the Statue of Liberty—'Give us your hungry...'"

"Work hard and play hard," said Simon as he remembered hearing stories about New Yorkers' eighty-hour workweeks. He was glad he didn't work there. He thought his sixty-hour workweek was long enough.

"Diversity," Georgia shouted out. "New York has such a diverse population."

"You are right about that," said Amanda. "Okay. I know we can come up with more values for New York. But let's think of a different city. What about Rio De Janeiro? What might their values be?"

"Maybe something like embracing natural beauty," said Melinda as she thought about how beautiful the city was with the beach and the mountains surrounding it.

"Sun and fun," said Georgia. She wondered what it would be like to live somewhere with warm weather every day, but she liked snow too much and immediately dismissed the idea.

"Colorful," said Simon. "Brazilian culture is very vibrant and energetic."

Amanda wrote all of their suggestions on the board, and then said, "Wonderful!"

"Are you saying cities are brands?" asked Melinda.

"That's a good question. I use cities as an example because

each city has a vibe, a culture, and a meaning. In this way, cities are like brands. Some cities attract more tourism and business than others, don't they? But it's different in the sense that cities don't necessarily have a brand steward that can truly create or influence its expression. Many people have a hand in the development of its culture and its values. In that way, it's not exactly a brand."

Amanda sees that the team somewhat buys her argument. She didn't share with the group her thoughts on the future of branding. In the future, Amanda believed that more brands were going to be created and co-opted by consumers, much like cities are, whereby brand stewards will invite consumers to participate in the brand's development. Conveying these novel ideas required a much longer conversation, and because there was so much more to do, she kept her thoughts to herself.

"So, what do we think? What are the values of Santa Claus?" she asks. "What are the values that the brand will live by?"

"I go back to the kids," says Melinda. "I think one of our values should be about kids and how we love and celebrate them."

Amanda writes down, "Celebrate Kids."

"That is an excellent one. I like that we should always consider the kids in everything we do," Amanda says.

"What about something we talked about before—wholesomeness?" asked Georgia. "That's why our sponsors like us. That's why parents like us. You won't find anything objectionable about Santa Claus."

"I like the word optimism," said Ethan. "I think we're

181

optimistic. The sun is always shining here, literally and figuratively."

Amanda laughed. She did notice that the sun rose much earlier and set much later in the evening than it did in New York. Almost eighteen hours of sunshine visited the North Pole each day this time of year.

"Giving," said Simon. "We are about giving." The executives all nodded their heads.

On the board were written the words: Celebrate Kids, Wholesomeness, Optimism, Giving.

Santa looked at the list and said, "Something is missing." He still had a nagging feeling that something just wasn't right. He thought about it for some time and then said, "Maybe we need to go back to the original vision for the Workshop...we were always about bringing joy. Can we put that in our values?"

"Of course," said Amanda, happy that Santa was feeling a little more comfortable with the work they were doing.

"To make sure we fully discuss our values, I want us to create a list of the values that we will fight for, and contrasting that, the values that we will fight against."

Amanda moderated the discussion on their values, and by the end of the talk, the Magic Paper revealed these words:

Fight For:
- We believe in kindness and doing good for others.
- We love to give. We believe giving is good for the soul.
- We are in the business of celebrating children.
- We are optimistic. We believe the future is very bright and beautiful.

- We aim to bring joy to the world.

Fight Against:
- We abhor meanness of any kind.
- We disdain stinginess or ulterior motives.
- We don't tolerate anyone who mistreats, abuses, or talks down to children.
- Nothing in life is ever hopeless, so pessimism has no place in our business.
- We don't like to see people unhappy. We want to spread smiles.

The executives debated the word "wholesomeness" for a long time and decided that it was better suited as a personality trait rather than a value. They went back to the brand blueprint and replaced "playful" with "wholesome," as it was a better fit with the brand personality. But they did add the word kindness to their values. They thought it was necessary because they wanted this to be part of the way they worked with each other.

Looking at the list of values they created, Amanda thought it captured the way the company wanted to operate. She congratulated them on completing their task. Then she pulled out magazines, scissors, markers, and glue sticks, and placed them in the middle of the table. "It's time for an art project."

CHAPTER 51
VISUALIZING THE BRAND

Most of the executives looked at each other with glee as they hadn't expected that they would be doing an art project as part of this brand work session. Simon shook his head and sat back in his seat with his arms crossed, "Is this necessary?" He had kept quiet most of the morning and tried to be a team player, but the art project felt a bit over the top to him.

Amanda looked at Simon, "I'm afraid so, Simon. And I appreciate your willingness to give this a try."

Ethan grabbed some markers and smiled, "I love drawing. I was a good artist as a kid, but my mom never let me draw at home after I got marker all over the walls."

"Well, you can draw all you want, Ethan," said Amanda. "Here's your assignment. I want you to create a visual representation of the brand. Look at the consumer portrait, review the brand blueprint, and read the values. These will inform the way you bring the brand to life."

Amanda instructed them to use the magazine photos and the markers to create a poster for the brand. She also had a few other art supplies in a bin that they could use if they felt inspired. Then she said, "I'll leave the room so you can work together in peace."

Wrapped in a warm sweater, Amanda went to get a breath of fresh air. She opened the front door of Santa's home and stood in the doorway, gazing out into the village square. She watched two elves on their break, who had decided to plop down onto the ground and make angels in the snow with their arms and legs.

Mrs. Claus, who was sweeping in the hallway, came to the open doorway and stood next to Amanda. "This is what Santa's Workshop is all about—magical moments like this," she said. She went back to her sweeping and disappeared around the corner into the kitchen.

Amanda wrapped her arms around herself as the cold wind blew into the doorway. She couldn't imagine living in a place that had winter all year round. But watching the elves playing in the snow, she understood why they loved the North Pole so much.

Amanda decided to go back inside and wait in the kitchen with Mrs. Claus. She enjoyed a steaming cup of hot tea as she waited for the executives to finish their assignment. She was tempted to check in on them to make sure they were on track, but she opted to leave them alone.

After forty-five minutes, Amanda went back into the room to check the status of the visuals, and what Amanda saw astonished her. The group had collaborated on a poster that perfectly captured the essence of Santa Claus. Red dominated the foreground, and the pictures were laid out into a box, just like a beautifully wrapped present. The images they had chosen were of happy children of all different nationalities, doing fun things together—like playing make-believe fairies, sledding down a hill, and opening presents.

The imagery was also of winter, capturing the season that seemingly visited the North Pole year-round. It was warm and inviting too; there was a photo of hot chocolate, a roaring fireplace, and a piece of warm apple pie. Red and silver glitter peppered the board. The team had thoughtfully brought the brand to life with imagery.

"Is this your handy work?" Amanda asked Ethan, pointing to the glitter.

"It is," Ethan said, beaming. "I got a little help too."

Amanda looked at Simon, who was standing nearby, his face with specks of glitter on it, his hands sticky with glue.

Across the left-hand side of the poster were the words: Wish, Hope, Dream, Rejoice.

Thrilled that they had chosen words that telegraphed the brand, she asked them to describe the visual identity in words. The team looked at the board and collectively came up with a list of words that described the look and feel of the brand. The words were: "Warm, Inviting, Red, Joyful, Vibrant." While some words also reflected the brand's personality, they appropriately described the visual cues of the brand as well.

Amanda beamed. "All of you, nice job. Especially you, Simon."

Simon smiled, thinking that the art project perhaps wasn't such a waste of time after all.

CHAPTER 52
THE NEW SANTA CLAUS HOTEL

"Now, we are going to take a field trip," said Amanda. She grabbed her coat and instructed everyone else to do the same.

Amanda led the group of executives across the village square and into the lobby of the Chocolate Hotel. Gathering them into a huddle, she spoke, "I was sitting in my bed last night thinking about the Santa Claus brand, and I looked around my room. It is certainly very beautifully designed, and it has a nice modern feel to it. Having furniture from contemporary designers, like Eames and Knoll, must be very impressive to your guests. And of course, when you walk into this lobby, it feels very indulgent. It smells like chocolate, and by gosh, its name is the Chocolate Hotel. No complaints from me, of course. I love chocolate." Amanda was feeling a bit provocative this morning. "But what do you think? Do you think this hotel reflects the essence of the Santa Claus brand?"

The executives looked around at the modern and brightly lit white lounge. Finally, Melinda spoke, "If we were totally honest with you, it's not very consistent with our brand. It is fun to have a place here with the latest design aesthetic, but it doesn't fit with our homey, warm persona."

"I think we need to 'Santa Claus' the hotel," exclaimed Santa.

"That's a great idea," said Amanda. "How would you do it?"

"Every room should have handmade quilt blankets," Georgia said. "The kind that Mrs. Claus makes."

"And big huge sleigh beds!" said Ethan with glee.

"Yes. I think the furniture should be antique and sturdy," Simon agreed.

"What about the lobby? What should the lobby look like?" Amanda asked.

"There should be a roaring fireplace." Melinda's eyes widened. "And a big comfy couch in front of it."

"I don't think we should get rid of the morning hot chocolate. That's yummy on a freezing day at the North Pole. And maybe we should serve apple pie, like in the photos," said Ethan, his mind already on lunch.

The rest of the executives nodded their heads in agreement.

"There should be a big spruce tree with little white lights on it. We should bring the outdoors in," said Santa.

"The walls should be red...tastefully red," Georgia said.

The hotel manager came over to the group of executives with a tray full of mugs. "Welcome, Santa. We haven't seen you in a while. How about a little hot chocolate to warm the soul?"

Standing in the middle of the lobby, the executives savored their hot chocolate in silence. It was a beautiful thing—a warm cup of hot chocolate on a brisk summer day.

CHAPTER 53
THE BRAND BLUEPRINT REVEALED

After their hot chocolate break, Amanda led the team back to the boardroom in Santa's home. When they all settled back down in their seats, she brought out the Magic Paper with a summary of the new brand blueprint they had developed over the last few days. The brand blueprint was now complete and brought to life with visuals.

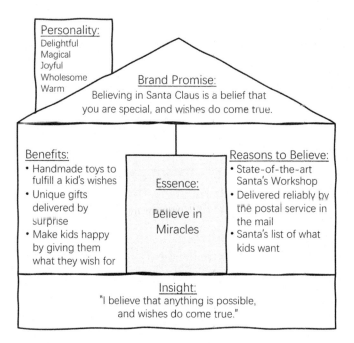

Personality:
Delightful
Magical
Joyful
Wholesome
Warm

Brand Promise:
Believing in Santa Claus is a belief that you are special, and wishes do come true.

Benefits:
• Handmade toys to fulfill a kid's wishes
• Unique gifts delivered by surprise
• Make kids happy by giving them what they wish for

Essence:
Believe in Miracles

Reasons to Believe:
• State-of-the-art Santa's Workshop
• Delivered reliably by the postal service in the mail
• Santa's list of what kids want

Insight:
"I believe that anything is possible, and wishes do come true."

"This is your brand blueprint. What do you think?" Amanda asked.

"This is awesome!" said Melinda. "I can see and feel the brand. It encapsulates the brand in a very concise way."

Georgia agreed. And she was thrilled that they weren't going to be making socks and underwear anymore.

"I can't wait to have apple pie at the hotel. If they use Mrs. Claus' recipe, it's going to be awesome," Ethan said.

"I feel like we've come a long way from where we were," said Simon.

Amanda could not tell if Simon was excited or lukewarm about the brand. But at least he thought they had made progress.

Santa cleared his throat. "I'm sorry, but something's missing. All the words are great, but I have a nagging feeling about this."

Amanda's heart skipped a few beats. All of a sudden, she saw Santa derailing the whole process. She took a deep breath and then asked, "Are there specific words you are getting caught up in?"

Santa looked at the words and thought for a long time. "I don't know."

Amanda stood back and re-read the words from the brand blueprint. She certainly felt that it was inspiring.

Santa read through the brand blueprint to himself. After a long pause, he finally spoke, "I guess it's the words: delightful and magical. I've been thinking about that little boy who was flying his truck around. He created the delight and magic for himself. We didn't create it for him."

The team sat in silence thinking about Santa's comment.

The boy, Tommy, who flew his truck in the air as his mother admonished him, had made an impression on the entire team.

All of a sudden, Amanda understood why Santa felt uneasy. "We could do better," she said. "I get it, Santa. You're right. We could be better at creating something delightful and magical for kids."

Just then, there was a hurried knock on the door, and Aidan, the Reindeer Master, rushed in. "Come quickly! Something amazing has just happened."

"What Aidan...tell us," Georgia said.

"You have to see for yourself. You wouldn't believe me if I told you," said Aidan as he began summoning each elf out of his or her seat. "Come on. Come on!"

Santa pushed himself out of his chair and started heading toward the door. The rest of the executives filed out of the boardroom after him, and Amanda followed behind the group.

CHAPTER 54

MIRACLE IN THE REINDEER BARN

When they got outside, Aidan ran in front of Santa, jumping sideways and backward, yelling, "You are not going to believe this," as he led them to the reindeer barn.

At the reindeer barn, Aidan opened the wooden doors. On a cushion of hay lay a baby reindeer, who had been born just moments before. The mother reindeer lay next to the baby, resting from the labor. Aidan's two caretakers, Christine and Alta, sat nearby watching the reindeer.

"Ho, Ho, Ho," laughed Santa. "A baby reindeer. How wonderful."

"Not any baby reindeer," said Aidan. "A special one."

As the baby reindeer woke up from his slumber, the group of executives hovered over him, smiling and cooing at the calf. He was so excited that his nose began to light up.

The group around him recoiled in surprise.

"His nose is red!" exclaimed Melinda.

"Shiny red!" added Simon.

"In all my years, I've never seen anything like this," said Santa. He kneeled over and touched the little reindeer's nose. "It's warm." He looked up at Aidan and asked, "What's this little feller's name?"

"The caretakers came up with a good one—Rudolph," answered Aidan.

"Rudolph," Santa repeated to himself softly. "Rudolph the red-nosed reindeer," he said out loud to the others.

Mumbling the new name of the reindeer to themselves, the executives smiled at the alliteration.

Santa petted Rudolph on his head. In the distance, through the barn doors, he could see the reindeer trainer, Ella, bringing in the other reindeer after their afternoon exercise. The group watched as Ella gently landed the reindeer and then trotted them toward the sleeping quarters adjacent to the barn.

"That's it!" exclaimed Santa. "I realize why the brand blueprint doesn't feel right! It's because we are magical, but we're not showing it to the kids."

"What do you mean?" asked Ethan.

"The reindeer...they are magical."

"Kids know all about the reindeer," said Melinda. "Almost every kid talked about it."

"Yes...but they don't ever get to see them as we do."

"I think it's good that there is a little mystery," said Aidan. "Plus, the reindeer don't like to be around too many big people. They get skittish."

"Santa's right," said Amanda. She thought about what Mrs. Claus said about Santa's Workshop being all about magical moments. "The magic of Santa Claus is real...but the actual experience of getting a present from Santa lacks magic."

Santa got up from the ground and pulled his suspenders to adjust his pants. "That's exactly right."

"Well, then, let's make the experience more magical for the kids."

"How do we do that?" Santa asked Amanda.

As the executives hovered over the red-nosed reindeer, they waited for Amanda to answer Santa's question.

"To describe that, I'll have to tell you about the Six Ps of brand marketing," said Amanda. "But first, can we close the doors to the barn? It's quite chilly in here."

Simon and Aidan went outside and pulled the large wooden barn doors closed. They dropped a large wooden plank across the framed doorway and then returned to the group huddled around the reindeer in the middle of the barn.

CHAPTER 55
THE SIX Ps

"**A**manda, what are the Six Ps?" asked Santa, eager to know how to improve the brand.

"The Six Ps stand for product, price, promotion, placement, people, and process," she answered. "By focusing on your Six Ps and excelling in the delivery of them, you will strengthen the brand experience." Then Amanda went on to explain each of the Six Ps in more depth.

"The first P is Product, or the actual item and its packaging. The product, in this case, is toys—the handmade toys developed and packaged by the elves." Then she challenged the executives, "How can you improve the products so that they better deliver on the brand blueprint?"

"I think the products are great," said Georgia. "They are high quality and made with only the best materials. And we are very innovative. We were the first ones to get into toy electronics, and now they're all the rage."

Ethan and Simon nodded their heads in agreement.

Melinda challenged the team. "I think it would be great to package the toys in colorful and fun wrapping paper. We have to use that brown wrapping paper because the post office wants it to look consistent. But I think we can make the experience of opening a gift much better. Not to mention, some of our consumers thought it was difficult to open."

"Maybe we could use ribbon and include a personal card from me," added Santa.

"That would be very expensive," said Simon as he calculated how much wrapping paper and ribbon would cost.

"Operationally, I don't think the post office will allow us to stray from the brown paper. Plus, if we added gift wrapping, production would slow down," Georgia said as she thought about how much the perfume line hampered production.

Amanda encouraged the group to think beyond costs right now. She wanted their best ideas on how to make the brand experience more magical. She knew that if they were creative, they'd find a way to make these product changes with minimal impact on costs and production.

Setting aside all the operational challenges and the fiscal implications, they all agreed that the changes to the product they discussed would undoubtedly enhance the product experience.

The next P was Pricing. "Pricing is how much the product costs to your consumers. But in the case of Santa's Workshop, the product is free to the consumer. In other cases, the pricing would be a big determinant of the brand experience. The perceived value that a consumer gets from the product, relative to the price, is an important distinction between brands. Some consumers are willing to pay a little more for higher quality while others are not. Figuring out your consumers' price threshold is an important part of designing a brand. For example, Fifer charges a premium for its hats due to their high-quality craftsmanship. Another elf favorite—the Jack Bean hat, on the other hand, costs half the price of Fifer hats because the brand targets younger elves and competes in the fashion accessory category," said Amanda.

The next P was Promotion or how a brand is promoted. "Promotion includes all the tools that marketers have at their disposal to get the message out about the brand, including marketing and advertising." Amanda listed some of the vehicles they could use to promote the brand. "These include television ads, print ads, licensing, direct mail, sponsorship, special events, and radio. Companies are developing new advertising methods all the time. Movie companies are now distributing their movies with advertisements before the feature film. A consumer can now watch a movie like *Love Bug* and see an advertisement for a Volkswagen Beetle."

They brainstormed ideas on how they could improve their promotion. They came up with an impressive list of ideas, including things like producing films and cartoons about the story of Santa Claus, hiring Santa Claus look-a-likes to sit in malls and take photos with kids, and conducting sweepstakes to win a trip to the North Pole. They liked some of the ideas generated but talked about the pros and cons of tourists coming to the North Pole. They agreed to continue the debate on all of the suggestions.

The next P stood for Placement. "This refers to the distribution and placement of the product, or its availability in different channels like grocery stores or department stores," Amanda said.

"We send our gifts through the mail, and it doesn't feel special. It's not magical," said Santa.

"But how else can we do it?" asked Simon. "It's the most cost-efficient way to send gifts."

The executives pondered the challenge: How else could they distribute the products? They looked around at each other. Santa caught Rudolph's smile, and he let out a little snicker. Rudolph's nose lit up.

Santa burst out, "By golly—the reindeer!"

Ethan instantly understood Santa's suggestion. "We can deliver them by reindeer!"

"Oh, my gosh," said Melinda. "That's brilliant!"

"Can we do that?" asked Georgia. She quickly added, "Of course, we can. We'll find a way to do it!"

"Who is going to deliver the gifts?" asked Amanda. "And how are you going to deliver them?"

Reindeer Master Aidan had been very quiet during the discussion, but he couldn't refrain from making a suggestion. "I don't know what you guys are doing, but I think it would be extraordinary if you delivered the gifts, Santa."

The rest of the group smiled in agreement.

"Me?" said Santa.

"That would be very special," said Melinda.

"And magical," said Ethan.

"That's a great suggestion, Aidan," praised Georgia.

"You know...doing it all in one day would be the most cost-effective way," suggested Simon.

"Amanda said we shouldn't do things just because it's the most cost-effective," Georgia said. "But I like the idea of doing it in one night because then kids can anticipate when they are getting the gift. And Santa, you could sneak down the chimney at nighttime and leave the gifts in their homes so in the morning they can wake up with a surprise—a wonderful gift by the fireplace."

"That's perfect!" said Santa. "That would be incredibly delightful for the kids."

"That would be delightful," agreed Amanda.

"It's a little dangerous. We'll have to get liability insurance," cautioned Simon.

"I'll be careful...and I can slip onto the roof with the reindeer sleigh and drop in and out in no time," he said.

"Maybe we should pick a night that's significant," added Melinda

"What about a day that means love?" suggested Georgia.

"Maybe a holy night," Ethan added.

"What about the night before Christmas?" said Santa. "That would be delightful!"

The others nodded in agreement.

"This is so wonderful...I can feel the brand coming alive!" exclaimed Santa.

The elves were so excited that they forgot that there were two more Ps left. Simon, who always focused on the numbers, didn't forget. "Amanda, what are the last two Ps?"

"Oh my...I almost forgot. I got so wrapped up in the moment," Amanda said. "The last two Ps are Process and People. The process is the way a company is organized to be able to deliver on the brand promise. It refers to everything from your supply chain to customer service, from human resources to facilities, and so on. Your entire enterprise needs to align with the brand promise and serve the needs of your consumers."

"The people part of the Six Ps means that you need to

have the right people in the right positions in service of the brand and its consumers," Amanda added.

"So, we should rethink our organizational processes and the people we have in place?" asked Santa Claus.

"Well, we are talking about completely reinventing the brand, so I think it would be worthwhile to discuss how to align the company around the vision," Amanda answered. She paused and then continued. "Just imagine how magical this brand could become by focusing on the Six Ps—product, price, promotion, placement, process, and people."

The group fell quiet as they thought about how unique the brand would be when they truly focused on fulfilling its brand promise through the Six Ps.

CHAPTER 56
THE NEW BLUEPRINT

"This is so great! Let's go back to the office and revise the brand blueprint right away," Amanda said.

The rest of the executives agreed, and they walked single file back to Santa's boardroom. As it was lunchtime, they walked rather briskly in anticipation of Mrs. Claus' food.

On the sideboard table in the boardroom, Mrs. Claus had left a sumptuous platter of thick, hearty Reuben sandwiches and a large New York-style cheesecake. Amanda looked at the lunch feast and began to think of how much she was going to miss the meals at the North Pole. They were the best corporate food she'd ever had, even after all the work she'd done for food companies.

Despite her hunger, Amanda worked as the others helped themselves to some food. She rewrote the brand blueprint and hung it up on the wall for everyone to study while they ate lunch. Then she helped herself to a generous sandwich and sank her teeth into it.

The executives sat around the table and studied the brand blueprint. It read:

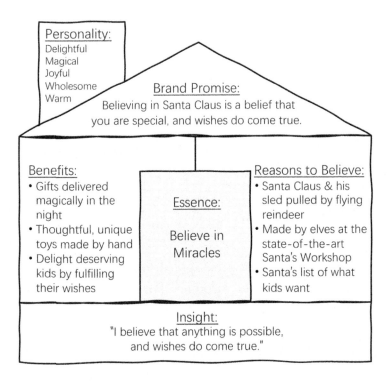

After everyone finished their meal, Amanda took them through all the material they had created. She read aloud their consumer portrait of the Wishful Optimists, reviewed the brand blueprint and the brand values, and held up their visual brand identity.

When Amanda finished reviewing the brand documents, the executives began clapping with joy. Even Simon clapped along cheerfully, whistling a few times to show his enthusiasm. It was the most animated Amanda had seen him. In fact, it was the most animated she had seen any of the executives. The executives felt joyful—satisfied knowing that they would not have to close down Santa's Workshop, happy they now had a direction for the brand, and glad that they were able to do it together.

Amanda joined the executives and clapped whole-heartedly. She had had her doubts that the team would be able to agree on the direction of the brand. In particular, she had worried that Santa's emotional investment in the Workshop would steer the team in the wrong direction and that Simon's negativity about the project would get in the way of the team's creativity. Despite these challenges, Amanda was able to get the team focused and aligned around a new vision.

Marveling at this remarkable and dedicated group, feeling proud of them for their commitment and passion, Amanda began to feel sad that her time at the Workshop was almost over. She only had one more thing to do with the team, and that was to prepare them to unveil the brand to the organization.

CHAPTER 57
THE LAUNCH

The executive team decided to hold the launch of the brand in a place that reflected the essence of Santa Claus. They spent a record two months completely redesigning the Chocolate Hotel into the Santa Claus Hotel. They brought in expert masons and designers to transform the modern hotel into a warm, cozy home, just as the executives had conceived it in the brand work session led by Amanda.

Invitations were sent out on toy cars that were wrapped in colorful wrapping paper and tied with curly ribbon. The card read:

Introducing the new Santa Claus brand
Join us at the newly redesigned Santa Claus Hotel
4 p.m., September 28, 1969
Bring your radiant smile!

❄ ❄ ❄

On the day of the grand unveiling, the executive team stood at the door and greeted the elves with exuberant cheers and high fives. Music reverberated throughout the hotel lobby; loudspeakers played a mix of songs created by elf musicians for the occasion. The musicians had been briefed on the new brand and had come up with cheerful songs that remain immensely popular today. Songs like "Santa Claus is Coming to Town" and "Rudolph the Red-Nosed Reindeer" had their debut on that particular day.

Next to a giant Douglas fir decorated with white lights was a stage with an enormous screen behind it. Projected on the screen were photos of kids from around the world. Some pictures featured kids playing with Santa's Workshop toys, while others showed kids having fun—like jumping in a pile of leaves or ice skating on a rink.

When the last of the elves filled the hotel lobby, the executives moved to the stage and got the crowd moving to the music. The place felt electrifying, and the elves were eager to hear what was in store for Santa's Workshop. Santa Claus' speech on the village square had eased their concerns, but now the elves wanted to know how the executives planned to turn around the Workshop. Even though Santa had promised that no one would lose their jobs, they were still apprehensive that their jobs would be affected by the management decisions. They waited with bated breath.

CHAPTER 58
SANTA'S RALLYING CALL

Santa took the stage wearing his traditional red, fur-lined suit and his red cap. He carried a big sack filled with wrapped presents and dropped it on the floor with a thump. Looking backstage to where his executives and Amanda, who had traveled to the North Pole for the unveiling of the brand, stood, he gave them a wink before addressing the audience.

"Welcome to the launch of the new Santa Claus brand. Are you feeling joyful?" he asked. He received a lukewarm "Yes" back from the audience.

"Once again...are you feeling joyful?" he shouted out.

The response was much stronger this time.

"Well, if you're not feeling joyful, hopefully by the end of this presentation, you will feel the joy again. Together we are here to reinvent Santa's Workshop. Your executive team and I put our heads together to think of how to bring joy back to the Workshop, how to grow the Workshop, and how to spread our vision. Through the help of a special lady, we began to realize that we needed to treat our company like a brand. We decided that we needed to refocus our efforts back on kids and to strengthen the emotional connection we have with our core consumer."

There were a lot of mumbles in the audience. Chef Milo, the perfumer, yelled out, "But what about the wonderful scents I just created?"

"Yes, I know that you are all concerned about what's going to happen to our adult lines, and most of all, your jobs. As I promised you, everyone will have a job. We will need to make some shifts in production. This recommendation doesn't come lightly. It comes with lots of work in understanding our consumer and our opportunity."

Santa turned to the screen. "You know. I can't say it better than these kids, so let's turn it over to them."

A film featuring kids and their thoughts of what brings them joy played on the large screen. It included audio that Amanda recorded from her tape recorder and images that Melinda had captured with her camera from the interviews. It featured a photo of Tommy flying his yellow truck. There were also sound bites of kids who called into the Workshop's call center and examples of letters that they received from around the world. The images and voices highlighted the key learning that kids believe anything is possible, and wishes do come true.

After the video, Santa described to the elves the idea of creating a cohesive brand built off of a consumer insight. Santa launched into a description of the target and the elements of the brand blueprint. He also described how they were going to change the brand's strategy and develop toys that he would personally deliver on Christmas Eve.

There were nods of approval and sighs of relief from many of the elves. But there were also some signs of disapproval.

"Christmas Eve is in three months!" exclaimed Elf

Hudson.

"Yes, I know. But with our focus on kids, we'll be able to fulfill many kids' wishes this year," Santa replied.

Oona yelled out, "What does this mean for the perfumes and the adult division?"

"That's a good question," retorted Santa. "We are shutting down these divisions, and we are going to retrain the staff so that we refocus on our core—toys for kids."

"But what about all that equipment?" yelled Clara.

"We've already found a buyer for the glass blowing unit in Toronto—an art gallery. And we are going to cut down the number of sewing machines to ten, and will sell the rest," Santa said. "We will use the proceeds from the sale of these items for retraining and consumer touchpoints."

"What does that mean?" yelled Elf Stella.

"It means that once a month we are going to have each elf sit on the consumer hotline to listen in on the conversations we have with kids. We will also make available all the consumer research we have done and will do in the future. We'll do regular readings of consumer letters in the village square. And several times a year, we will bring a lucky set of consumers up to the Workshop to help us develop and test new toys."

"They're not the experts...we are," yelled the train builder Kiley.

"Oh, contraire, my friend. They are absolutely the experts. They are the ones we are designing our products for, and they should have a say in the development of the products," Santa said. "We should be truly grateful to them. These kids are what we are all about. It's time that we listen to them."

Amanda watched Santa advocate on behalf of the children. She felt so proud that he put kids front and center in his business. As Santa continued speaking about the kids they would be targeting, Simon came up to Amanda.

"I wanted to tell you that I appreciate your work," said Simon as he shuffled his feet. "I was dubious. I'm not going to lie. But I feel like we are in a better place. So, thank you." Simon reached out his hand for Amanda to shake.

Amanda took his hand, pulled Simon towards her, and wrapped her arms around him. The unexpected hug made Simon stiffen at first, but after feeling Amanda's warm embrace, he hugged her back.

"Thank you for trusting me," whispered Amanda into his ear before pulling back.

They both turned their attention back to Santa on stage.

"We also want to create a culture here where your ideas are valued," said Santa. "We are going to hold new product sessions to get better at innovation. We'll also have an 'Idea Sled' in the middle of the workshop so that you can submit your toy ideas. The elves will vote on the best innovation, and then we'll put that idea into development. The elf who comes up with the winning idea gets to accompany me on Christmas Eve to deliver the packages to the kids that year."

A wave of excited "ahs" swept across the audience.

"Finally, of course, we still have our corporate sponsors to nurture. We are creating a task force to make sure that we meet the needs of our sponsors, and that they have access to our learning about our kids. We know that if we keep our kids happy, we'll keep them happy as well."

CHAPTER 59

BRAND METRICS

Continuing his formal presentation, Santa unveiled the structural changes and metrics for the organization.

First, there were a few critical changes in the leadership of the organization. Melinda kept her position as liaison to the corporate sponsors. "But she will also be in charge of all consumer research so that we are constantly up-to-date on changes in the marketplace," Santa said. "Georgia will take on a new role as brand and innovation director to make sure that we are consistent in all our communications and new product initiatives," Santa continued. Ethan remained in his function as human resources director, with the added role of education coordinator, ensuring that all elves maintained an excellent understanding of their consumers. And Simon remained in his position as finance director.

With all the changes to the organization announced, Santa posted a chart and declared to his elves that he was committed to reaching the following goals:

SANTA'S WORKSHOP DASHBOARD YEAR 1
Employee Satisfaction: 90%
Productivity: +200%

Sponsorship Income: Flat
Returns by Consumers: 0%
Positive to Negative PR Articles: 200/10
Brand Awareness: 90%

He knew that these goals were aggressive, but he was confident that with the changes they were making, he could get his employee satisfaction levels up to ninety percent and then back to one hundred percent in a few years. As a result of the changes in production, Santa believed the company could return to levels of productivity before the crisis. Other goals included stopping corporate sponsors from leaving and deterring consumer returns. Then there were other measures about the health of the brand that he wanted to start measuring. The company had never monitored their media coverage and brand awareness levels before, and Santa knew this would be valuable information to track.

The new dashboard criteria seemed to spark public debate by the elves, which Santa gladly addressed. He was committed to putting metrics down so that the company could monitor its progress. While the parameters might change once they were out of their precarious business situation, these were the metrics he felt would help the company stay focused on revitalizing the business.

Santa stood at the podium in the hotel and patiently answered all the elves' questions about the new brand organization. The elves began to feel comfortable with the new direction of the company, and the energy of the room shifted from apprehension to optimism. After Santa addressed all of the audience questions, he made one last pitch to his employees, "A new day has dawned on Santa's Workshop. We are a family, and our biggest commitment is to these kids. Let's help bring more smiles to the world. Thank you."

With those inspiring words, the elves stood up and began cheering for Santa. "SAN-TA, SAN-TA!" Santa had never experienced such an outburst of support and emotion. His eyes began to tear as he felt a deep sense of gratitude in his heart. He looked over at Amanda, who stood backstage. She smiled at Santa as her eyes welled up with tears. She gave him a thumbs-up before joining the rest of the audience in chanting his name "SAN-TA, SAN-TA."

CHAPTER 60
CHRISTMAS EVE

Santa slipped his red pants over his big belly and smoothed out his white shirt before tucking it into his pants. He gently pulled his red suspenders over his shoulders and tightened the straps. Looking at his reflection in the mirror, he smiled and then tugged at his suspenders. His heart fluttered with excitement and anticipation for his second flight around the world.

Doll maker Julie watched Santa from the cracked door to his bedroom. She cleared her throat to make herself known to Santa. He turned around.

"Oh, Julie," said a startled Santa. "Are you ready for the trip?" he asked as he put on his furry, red coat and began buttoning it.

"Yes, yes, yes, of course! They are ready for us, and we should get going," Julie uttered, hardly able to contain herself. It would be her first flight around the world, and it felt like a childhood dream come true.

"I'll be there in a moment," Santa replied as he buckled his black belt. He turned to look at Julie, but the little elf had disappeared as quickly as she had appeared.

Santa gave out a chuckle. He understood how Julie felt. He had flown his first global reindeer flight last Christmas Eve, and it was exhilarating. It was intoxicating to be a part of something so special. He sat down in his armchair and put on his boots, carefully tucking his pants into the lip of the shoes.

He took one final look in the mirror. He smoothed out his beard and looked at his reflection, remembering how his mother always told him to dress nicely before any monumental event. "I look very good if I do say so myself," he said to himself. He gave out a belly laugh, "Ho, ho, ho."

He reached for the red hat that was lying on top of his dresser and pulled it over his head until it felt snug.

"Well," he said to his reflection in the mirror. "It's time to go and spread some happiness to some deserving kids."

Santa arrived with Mrs. Claus at the reindeer barn as the last of the gifts were loaded onto the sleigh. All of the inhabitants of the North Pole had come to see Santa off for his trip. Julie nervously walked around the vehicle, checking to make sure it was in peak condition for their flight.

"Don't worry, Julie," reassured Santa. "The sleigh is in great condition. Graham, the mechanic, does a thorough check. It's designed to fly the entire night and then some."

Santa walked toward the reindeer, who stood two by two in their harnesses, attached by reins. Starting from the back, he gave an encouraging word and a pat to each of the reindeer. First Dasher and Dancer, Prancer and Vixen. Then Comet, Cupid, Donner, and Blitzen. Finally, he came to the smallest and youngest of the reindeer, Rudolf. He patted Rudolf on the head and asked the little reindeer, "Are you ready to lead us?" Rudolf's red nose lit up the barn as if to say, "Ready as I'll ever be."

Santa gave out a big belly laugh. "Well, let's get going then!"

CHAPTER 61
AND TO ALL A GOOD NIGHT

After giving Mrs. Claus a goodbye kiss, Santa walked over to the sleigh and climbed in. Julie jumped into the sleigh, taking the rear to watch over the bags of gifts. She felt proud to be the one chosen out of all the elves in the company to accompany Santa. Her new dancing funk doll won that year's innovation contest. Funk was sweeping across the world, and Julie was astute enough to notice this new trend. She created a doll that sported silver lamé and platform shoes and danced funk moves to the tunes of James Brown and Sly & the Family Stone. Six hundred little girls would receive the doll for Christmas that year.

Santa grabbed the reins of the sleigh and put them on his lap. A feeling of exhilaration overcame him. A year and a half ago, the Workshop was on the brink of failure. His ego clouded his judgment, and he had lost sight of his initial vision to bring joy to kids around the world. He felt so grateful to Amanda and his executive team for helping him create a brand-led company. If it weren't for them, the Workshop might not have survived the crisis.

When he looked into the crowd, he saw his faithful leaders: Georgia, Simon, Melinda, and Ethan. They were standing beside the sleigh and clapping and cheering as they had done the year before—the night of Santa's first Christmas Eve flight.

Earlier that day, Simon told Santa the excellent news. They exceeded all of his dashboard metrics over the last year. Today, employee satisfaction was a solid one hundred percent. Productivity was at an all-time high, and they had produced two million toys for deserving kids around the world that year. Not only did they stabilize their sponsorship income, but they also added two new sponsors into their family, which helped them pay for their consumer programs and the production of more innovative toys. There were no returns from kids last year, and they expected the same this year.

As for public relations, the re-launch of the Santa Claus brand was a smashing success. On Christmas Day the first year, 2,475 articles ran in the late-day edition of local newspapers and magazines about the surprising gifts that showed up next to fireplaces around the world. Santa had a tremendously positive effect on happiness levels around the world. More than 821 articles about Santa's kindness and generosity followed that year. The world had fallen back in love with Santa Claus.

Melinda wanted to make sure that they had a systematic way to track the brand's health. She commissioned an esteemed global research company to develop a survey that would track kids' perceptions of Santa Claus. Melinda worked with the research firm to implement a brand tracking study—a comprehensive quantitative survey with kids that measured specific brand measures like their affinity to Santa Claus. By tracking this every quarter, the company could address any significant negative shifts promptly.

Before she left the North Pole, Amanda cautioned the company not to rest on its laurels. She told the team that they must keep abreast of shifts in consumer attitudes, cultural trends, and competitive threats. They must be ready to react if any of these factors began affecting their brand perceptions, and they must be willing to revisit their brand strategy.

Santa sat as the cheers around him grew louder and louder. He turned to Julie, who had settled into the back seat and asked, "Are you ready to spread joy?"

Julie yelled, "Yes!" But, Santa could barely hear her voice over the noise.

Santa flicked his wrists upward, sending a wave across the reins that he held tightly in his hands. The reindeer walked forward slowly at first, then transitioned to a quick trot. The light from the barn glowed and formed a crescent along the adjacent field. With a slight jerk the sleigh started to ascend into the luminescent night with the reindeer leading the way. The cheers from the elves grew louder. As the reindeer galloped into the night air, Santa looked back at the barn and let out a loud "Ho, ho, ho."

Santa pulled on his rein once more, and the reindeer began galloping faster and higher into the air. The sounds of the elves below grew more distant. The full moon shined brightly in the sky, and the night air was crisp and delicious. Santa Claus shouted for the world to hear, "Ho, ho, ho. Merry Christmas to all, and to all a good night."

EPILOGUE

I'd be remiss if I didn't make a few broad statements about the use of this book. First, it's important to note that marketing is part art and part science. There are no right or wrong answers, and not every marketing strategy developed will succeed. What I've outlined for you is a process by which you can think about your business. There are no hard and fast rules about how to go about this process. Much of it is trial and error. I've had my fair share of mistakes in marketing. But, with a disciplined approach to branding, combined with creativity and a small leap of faith, you'll have a better shot at making your brand stand out from the rest.

In my made-up world, Santa's Workshop is a hybrid non-profit. It funds its business through the sale of licenses. I've included a commercial and a non-profit aspect in the story, so it is relatable to all types of organizations. Please don't let this throw you off. There may be many differences between your organization and Santa's Workshop (in terms of the consumers, competition, and context), but the same marketing principles hold. The process you go through is the same, whether you are a for-profit or a non-profit organization. It's the same whether you market a product or a service, or whether you market to consumers or businesses. Furthermore, in using Santa's Workshop as my model company, I'm not advocating that you become seasonal producers and sell your product in one night. Using this example is merely a way to illustrate that you need to align your brand around your consumers. You must start with a compelling insight and build a brand that stays true to your consumer and your brand promise. Compelling insights will help you develop a clear direction to take your brand. And a relentless commitment to your consumer and your brand will help you both retain your loyal consumers and grow your brand.

Because everything starts with consumer insights, I wanted to make a few comments about research. There are many types of research available, in-home interviews being only one example. Different approaches include focus groups, quali-quant studies, mobile research, intercepts, observations, and the list goes on. To determine the best approach, there are many factors to consider, including the research objectives, timing, and budget. If you are on a micro-budget, you can DIY your approach and find appropriate respondents through business associates and friends of friends. The important thing is to find the right people and ask the right questions.

I also wanted to make a few comments about the use of the brand blueprint. First, don't get hung up on the fact that it is laid out in the shape of a house. One of my clients decided to draw it as a brownstone because it felt appropriate for the brand. It doesn't matter if it looks like a house, a flower, a square, or any number of different shapes. What matters is that it captures the essential components, mainly the consumer insight, benefits, reasons to believe, personality, brand promise, and brand essence.

I did not "invent" the brand blueprint. Most disciplined consumer packaged goods companies have some type of brand marketing tool. Many of these tools contain similar material—except they come in different shapes, like keys, triangles, diamonds, wheels, compasses, etc. You get my point. Make the tool your own and use it in a way that best serves you and your organization.

The brand blueprint and the tools I've outlined in this book serve as strategy documents to guide in brand development. Whether you are creating a new brand or repositioning an existing brand, you can use these tools to brief designers or agency partners when creating your brand identity, website, or brand communications. You may have some specific communications objectives for your brand, such as introducing a new product feature or illuminating a competitive advantage, which may necessitate the use of additional briefing tools like a packaging or an advertising brief.

You might be wondering why I set this book in 1969. It was a creative choice that felt culturally relevant for my readers and served the story theme. 1969 was both a tumultuous and inspiring year in the United States, the country where I was born and raised. By placing the story in 1969, it means that this book doesn't cover the massive explosion of the Internet and the advent of digital marketing and social media. Social media is one of the many ways to activate the brand, just like advertising and promotions, and is an important way for your brand to engage with your consumers. In the future, new mediums will be invented, and those may become just as important as social media is today. The point is, keep abreast of new and innovative ways to engage with your consumer as it will continually evolve.

In the story, I did not try to explain branding principles with examples from the real world. I wanted you to be immersed in the story of Santa Claus and learn from the examples I provided from the North Pole—namely Mrs. Claus' beef stew and Fifer hats. You can find some real-world brand examples on www.santasboardroom.com, where you can also find worksheets that will help you create a brand blueprint.

While this book is about marketing, it also highlights a few things about leadership. In the story, I've tried to illuminate what it means to be a good leader and how to steward a team effectively. To turn around his business, Santa needed to learn to listen to his consumers and his employees. As a brand leader, you must be clear and precise in your mission. You must learn to trust the expertise of the people you've put in place to run the business and trust in the value of teamwork to solve challenging problems.

To be a great brand steward, I believe it's important to approach branding in a disciplined manner, using consumer insights to guide you and an understanding of the market realities to inform your decisions. By using the branding tools I've outlined in the story, I hope that you are able to better define your brand and meet the needs of your consumers. Happy branding to all, and to all, good luck!

ACKNOWLEDGMENTS

My sincere gratitude goes to everyone who helped in the creation of this book. Thank you to Julie Mak, Chris Jacobs, Christine Durkin, Alexis Lee, Shawn Kolitch, and Leah Brown for your help on various aspects of this book. Claudia Rose, I'm lucky to have you as my friend and writing cheerleader. To the former members of the First Friday consulting group, thank you for your input when this book was just an idea.

Throughout my career, I've been blessed to have worked with many brilliant marketers. It all started when I took my first marketing class at Half Hollow Hills High School East on Long Island. Thank you, Mr. Burns, for inspiring me to begin my journey into marketing. I am grateful to my mentors and co-workers for their guidance and collaboration through the years. While there are too many to name here, know that I appreciate you. As real work sessions inspired this book, I must also thank my clients for their trust and partnership.

I'd also like to thank my mother and father, and my sisters, Jennifer and Julie, for their constant and unwavering love and support. My deepest gratitude goes to my partner

Andy, who encouraged me to write this book and also made beef stew for me while finishing it. And finally, thank you to the countless kids in my life who have inspired the characters in this book, including my daughter, Ella; my nieces, Amanda, Andi, and Oona; and my nephews, Elijah, Ethan, Jacob, Aidan, Aaron, and Milo.

ABOUT THE AUTHOR

Lisa S. Lee is a writer, brand strategist, and founder of Lila & Company, where she works with companies and agencies to grow their brands through communications, innovation, and training. Before starting Lila & Company, she was a brand and innovation manager at Unilever, an advertising planner at BBDO, and a strategist at Redscout. She has worked on a variety of brand challenges for companies such as PepsiCo, L'Oreal, Johnson & Johnson, and SC Johnson, as well as smaller firms and start-ups. Lisa attended Tufts University and Kellogg Graduate School of Management at Northwestern University, and currently lives with her family in Portland, Oregon. You can learn more about her company at www.lilaandcompany.com and her writing at www.lisaslee.com.

Printed in Great Britain
by Amazon

29392448R00126